Selling
Out the
Church

Selling Out the Church

The Dangers of Church Marketing

Philip D. Kenneson & James L. Street

Abingdon Press
Nashville

SELLING OUT THE CHURCH

Copyright © 1997 by Abingdon Press

This book is printed on recycled, acid-free paper.

Library of Congress Cataloging-in-Publication Data

Kenneson, Philip D.
    Selling out the church : the dangers of church marketing / Philip D. Kenneson & James L. Street.
        p. cm.
      Includes bibliographical references.
      ISBN 0-687-01044-6 (pbk. : alk. paper)
      1. Church marketing—Controversial literature.   I. Street, James
L.   II. Title.
    BV652.23.K46   1997
    254'.0068'8—dc21   96-53658
                                    CIP

97 98 99 00 01 02 03 04 05 06 — 10 9 8 7 6 5 4 3 2 1

MANUFACTURED IN THE UNITED STATES OF AMERICA

For Kim and Linda

CONTENTS

ACKNOWLEDGMENTS

W RITING A BOOK TOGETHER HAS IN many ways been more difficult than either of us imagined. While not as laborious, time consuming, or frustrating as writing a committee report, writing together requires the development of habits different from those needed for writing alone (if such a practice actually exists). But working together has also been enormously beneficial, not least because we have often found ourselves being forced to articulate more clearly what seemed obvious to only one of us. It seems unlikely that we would have undertaken to write this book had we not been good friends. For that abiding and sustaining friendship, which is largely rooted in many shared convictions, we give thanks to God, by whose providence our lives were brought together.

It would be misleading, however, to suggest that this book is simply the product of two friends from East Tennessee. We are grateful for the generous help and insight offered to us by numerous colleagues, friends, and pastors, many of whom read and commented on early drafts of the manuscript, while others responded to queries about specific matters. We would like to thank Randal Barnhart, David Chadwick, Inagrace Dietterich, Wes Dillon, L. Gregory

Jones, Kim Kenneson, Thomas Langford, Frederick Norris, Calvin Phillips, Allan Poole, Bruce Shields, Linda Street, Charles Taber, and John Wade. We extend our thanks as well to Stanley Hauerwas, who read and commented on our book more than once and graciously accepted Abingdon's invitation to write the foreword. We owe a special debt of gratitude to Margaret Adam and Andrew Adam, who not only made our manuscript a topic of family conversation over a period of many months, but also offered numerous substantive and editorial suggestions that improved both the book's argument and its readability.

Part of the research for and writing of this book was made possible by a sabbatical leave granted to Jim by Milligan College. For the past four years our offices at Milligan have been across the hall from each other, which has greatly facilitated ongoing conversations about these and other matters. The completion of this book coincides with a transition for Jim, who is leaving both his pastorate of fourteen years and his office at Milligan College to assume new responsibilities at the graduate seminary across the street, Emmanuel School of Religion.

We have dedicated this book to two women who over the years have supported our vocations in innumerable ways and sustained our very existence with countless acts of grace.

Stanley Hauerwas

OR THOSE OF US WHO ARE IDENTIFIED with what might be called the "high culture" institutions of American Protestantism, church marketing is ignored as somehow beneath our purview. Indeed, church marketing often looks like a movement that only Kurt Vonnegut could have imagined. Yet this movement is real and few developments are having greater effect on the actual practice of the church than those advocating and writing about church marketing. For example, if any of us writes a book in theology, it might sell five thousand copies at best. Books in church marketing sell in the tens of thousands. Clearly, we ignore this significant development at our own and the church's peril.

We are, therefore, in the debt of Kenneson and Street for the care with which they have read the literature of those promoting church marketing as a technique. We are even more in their debt for the way they have exposed the theological presuppositions that inform the marketing project. Kenneson and Street help us see that the marketer's presumption that form can be separated from the content of the gospel betrays an understanding of the gospel that cannot help betraying the gift that is Christ. Of course, no one is more damaged by the assumption that marketing is

11

"only" a technique than those who advocate the marketing of the church. The very language of technique betrays the perverse character of marketing, since the very presumption that ends and means can be separated reproduces the manipulative strategies so characteristic of modernity. Such strategies, as Alasdair MacIntyre has argued, result in the substitution of the expert for the disciple.

This is not, however, simply a book of criticism. Critical though they are of the marketing strategy, Kenneson and Street just as importantly develop a constructive account of "practical theology." Their position is based not on exchange but on reminding us that the gospel is always a gift—a gift, moreover, that makes impossible any presumption that there can be an exchange between human beings and God that is rooted in the satisfaction of our untrained needs. Rather, what the gift of God's life does for the church is to transform our needs into service. In short, God makes us disciples through cross and resurrection in a way that challenges the world's understanding of what our needs should be.

That we exist as God's people by gift is a reminder that we also live as Christians by memory. Yet, according to Kenneson and Street, so much of the marketing literature about the church is based on an attempt to make us forget who we are as God's people. As Christians we live through the witness of the saints, whose memory is precious to us, because they make our lives possible. The church that seeks to meet the undisciplined needs of people is not a church that lives by memory; rather, it is a church that underwrites the presumption that our needs and wants require no justification beyond the fact that they are our needs and wants.

The marketing of the church is often done by those who think of themselves as religiously conservative and in the name of preserving "moral values." Ironically, however, we discover through Kenneson and Street's analysis that religious conservatives share much with Protestant liberals just to the extent that they accept an anthropological starting point for their understanding of the Christian faith. Both assume that Christianity is meaningful just to the extent that what Christians believe depends for its intelligibility on satisfying or resolving some account of the human condition. Accordingly, it never seems to occur to those who put forward marketing as a strategy for "bringing people back to Christ" that the Christ to whom we are brought back has very little to do with the one who would require our very lives if we are to be faithful to his cross. In short, religious conservatives and religious liberals are equally confounded by the old Calvinist question: "Are you ready to be damned for the glory of God?"

It is a remarkable feature of this book that Kenneson and Street do not write in a strident fashion. They do not personally attack any of those advocating church marketing. They recognize that these are good and concerned people. They also understand that those advocating church marketing, like all of us, are caught in a market society. Indeed, one of the great agonies is how one does learn to avoid the market. For example, the very fact that Abingdon Press is publishing this book along with many books by church marketers suggests that Abingdon cannot help continuing the presumptions of those who advocate the market. Of course, it is one thing to market books and quite something else to market the church. Yet the very fact that Abingdon has published Kenneson and Street's book seems to suggest that what the marketers advocate is unavoidable even for God.

The melancholy truth that Kenneson and Street put forward in this book acknowledges that the market has extraordinary power. Indeed, the market has all the characteristics of a Pauline power. Yet they also give us hope that we who desire to be faithful followers of Christ, the Christ who defeated the powers, have been given the means to defy those powers. That they have written such a serious and important book about a topic that might be otherwise ignored is at least the beginning of an alternative.

CHAPTER ONE

The Frog in the Kettle

MARKETING THE CHURCH IS HOT. AN acquaintance of ours from California recently remarked that for many congregations in his state, marketing the church is the first article of the creed. Is this merely another California fad? We don't think so. Granted, most Christians would cringe at the suggestion that creedal status be given the idea that the church should rethink its identity and mission with the aid of marketing strategies and tactics. But plenty of congregations are showing deep interest in exploring how marketing techniques can help them be more effective.

The reasons for this interest are clear. Many Christians rightly sense that the church is a marginal factor in the lives of most Americans, and even of many self-identified Christians. Many believe that the church is increasingly irrelevant, that it has failed to keep up with the times, that it no longer addresses people's perceived needs. For those who name the church's problems in such terms, marketing philosophy looks like a godsend. These persons look out at the business world and see marketing's impressive ability to create and to maintain markets around the globe, and they reasonably ask: "Might such techniques be used to save the church from slipping into utter irrelevance and oblivion?"

The answer from many quarters seems to be a resounding, "Yes!" Many churches have self-consciously adopted a marketing orientation and have experienced (sometimes remarkable) numeric and programmatic growth. Many others have been far less systematic about adopting such techniques, but have found themselves operating from similar assumptions about the nature of the church and its mission. We want to offer some words of caution in the following pages. We believe that the issue is not simply whether marketing principles and techniques can be used effectively to draw "unchurched" people to a worship service or to create a support group for men with midlife crises, as commendable as these activities might be. The more fundamental issue concerns the impact a marketing orientation has on the church's self-understanding and mission. Put as starkly as we know how, the question is, Can the market-driven church remain Christ's church?

There are no quick, easy answers to that very important question. Instead, congregations need patiently to consider both the benefits and the dangers of adopting a marketing orientation. Understandably, advocates of church marketing spend the bulk of their energy touting the benefits of church marketing. We hope to enable a more robust debate about the wisdom of employing church marketing by articulating as clearly as we can what we take to be its dangers. Unfortunately, some church marketers believe that there is very little left to debate.

> For the most part, the debate is over. Although the need is always there to be held accountable for our actions and our motives, and to conscientiously avoid compromising any portion of biblical truth, the church is better off in every way when it blends good marketing practice with unswerving commitment to the call of Christ.[1]

We hope the debate is not over, for we think there are good reasons to believe that this "blend" is detrimental to the long-term health of the church. To see why this is true requires patient reflection—reflection we think is still in its early stages.[2] So consider the following pages as a contribution to what we hope is a churchwide conversation about the identity, character, and mission of the church, and more specifically about the wisdom of employing marketing thinking and practices in the service of that church.

We think it important to say up front that we do not question the sincerity or motives of church-marketing advocates. They, like us, care deeply about the church. Moreover, we deeply respect the abiding concern many advocates of a marketing orientation demonstrate for reaching "unchurched" people in our society. But we do have deep differences, and these differences are not merely about which strategies best serve the church. Indeed, our dispute with church marketers is most accurately characterized as a fundamental disagreement about the very identity, character, and mission of the church itself.

This should not be surprising. We believe that many Christians and non-Christians alike are understandably confused about the purpose of Christ's church. As we will see, one of the claimed benefits of church marketing is a clearer vision of the church's mission. Although we do not want to deny that this could happen, we do worry that the image of the church that marketing philosophy presupposes and the kind of church that marketing practice helps to create are seriously distorted. We mention several images here—several that church marketers openly embrace and others that are underwritten by their practice if not by their theory—so that readers will recognize them when they are taken up in subsequent chapters.

1. The Entrepreneurial Church. In this model, the church is viewed primarily as a business, as one more organization (albeit "religious") whose task is to take risks and create ("spiritual") profit by offering certain "products." As one group of church marketers claims, if churches fail to become entrepreneurial and more professional, they are in danger of becoming "religious museums."[3]

2. The Instrumentalist Church. An instrumentalist philosophy encourages us to ask of everything: What is it good for? For example, an instrumentalist view of the world encourages us to see trees as lumber, animals as food, and people as a labor force. An instrumentalist view of the church encourages people to see it as an institution for meeting predetermined needs. For example, the church is valuable, in this view, because it strengthens family relationships, gives a sense of meaning and purpose, and offers people an experience of community. Such instrumentalism also underwrites the next four related images of the church, all of which are preoccupied with the "What's it good for?" question.

3. The Relevant Church. Much of the current discussion about the church focuses on its seeming irrelevance to the everyday lives of contemporary men and women. Many insist that this perceived irrelevance is at the heart of the church's declining prestige and influence. Advocates of church marketing suggest that the church could regain this lost status if it would be willing to "repackage" itself in ways that are more attractive and relevant to the average customer.

4. The Self-interested Church. People have argued for a long time whether humans are capable of genuinely altruistic behavior. Church marketing considers it axiomatic that people act primarily on the basis of self-interest. Since this is the case, the church that desires to attract new members must clearly articulate the benefits of membership to potential members. In marketing terms, the church must clearly understand itself as being in the business of managing self-interested, yet mutually beneficial, exchanges.

18

5. The Full-service Church. Within the entrepreneurial framework, the question arises as to what kind of business the church is in. Advocates of church marketing encourage the church to view itself as a service agency. As one group writes: "Religious organizations exist to be responsive to the needs of their members and constituents, and responsive to the needs of society. A responsive congregation is one that makes every effort to sense, serve, and satisfy the needs and wants of its members and participants within the constraints of its budget."[4]

6. The Therapeutic Church. Several commentators on life in the United States have noted that ours is a therapeutic society.[5] We expend enormous amounts of energy and resources to "feel better about ourselves" or to rebuild our self-esteem. In a society in which such activities have become the central preoccupation and are viewed as self-justifying (that is, no one asks *why* we ought to feel better about ourselves), it seems natural to expect the church to offer this therapeutic service. When church marketers research the needs of their potential consumers, such therapeutic needs are often at the forefront. Thus it comes as no surprise that the most popular reason people give for joining the proliferating number of support groups that churches offer in the name of ministry is "to feel better about themselves."[6]

7. The Forgetful Church. Words like *tradition* and *traditional* are not popular with many religious consumers steeped in the culture of novelty. Although those words can often be synonymous with "the way we've always done things," they can also be a much needed pointer to the two-thousand-year-old heritage of the church, a heritage that congregations fixated on the "contemporary" ignore to their detriment. Sadly, the result is often a church that has forgotten the purpose for which it has been called into existence. Church marketing, by focusing on the contemporary needs of its potential consumers, often contributes unwittingly to this amnesia.

8. The Ephemeral Church. As noted above, church marketing encourages the church continually to repackage itself in order to be fully responsive to the needs and wants of religious consumers. In a society where much of people's lives is ordered by the logic of consumer exchanges, marketing serves two purposes: It caters to the desires people currently have, and it stimulates novel desires, because consumers well understand their power in a market economy to demand that their as yet unmet needs be addressed. This creates an environment in which people's perceived needs and wants are constantly changing. As a result, the church that wraps its identity and mission around the evanescent desires of finicky consumers will run the risk of creating a church as ephemeral as those desires.

9. The Engineered Church. People in western cultures are often justly accused of being "control freaks." We like to think that we are largely in control of our circumstances, or at least that we could be if we used the proper techniques. Church marketing embodies such an attitude, for it presents itself as a technique for "outreach" or "evangelism," yet it does so by suggesting that the church is engaged in little more than engineering or managing mutually beneficial exchanges. Armed with these techniques, churches are mistakenly encouraged to think (to paraphrase a line from *Field of Dreams*) that "if you engineer it, they will come." All church marketers claim that they leave room for the working of the Spirit, but too often this seems to amount to little more than asking God to bless what they have already engineered on strictly human terms.

10. The Homogeneous Church. It has long been a truism that 11:00 Sunday morning is the most segregated hour of the week. That churches in the United States are divided along racial, ethnic, political, and social class lines is hardly news. Church marketing, by unapologetically catering to what makes people "comfortable," encourages congregations to target relatively homogeneous groups in the name of more efficient outreach. The result is often even more homogeneous churches that call into question the power of the gospel to break down social barriers.

11. The Pragmatic Church. Americans have a reputation for being fundamentally pragmatic. Few of us can resist the temptation to ask of almost everything: "But does it work?" As a result, heading the list of virtues we most deeply respect and desire is "effectiveness." Certainly, part of the allure of church marketing is that it promises to make us more effective.[7] But too often effectiveness becomes its own end. Too rarely do we press on to inquire: Effective in doing what? Are the goal and purpose of the church simply to "serve people more effectively"? If so, then church marketing will be enormously helpful; if it is not, then its tendency to focus on the pragmatic may encourage the church to forget the importance of faithfulness. We believe that the faithful church can be effective at serving God's purposes; we are not convinced that the "effective" church need be faithful.

12. The Christendom Church. For fifteen hundred years, the church in the West developed certain expectations about its role in society. For much of that time, the church's status, influence, and agenda were underwritten by the powers that be. In contrast to the early years of the church, when it took great courage to be a Christian, Christendom created a situation in which it required great courage not to be a Christian. Hence, in an era when most people were regarded as Christians, the language of "church" came to refer less and less to a distinctive and visible assembly of believers and more and more to structures, hierarchies, and buildings whose visibility far surpassed that of the Body of Christ. Indeed, in many cases these institutions were regarded as more "church" than the people of God were. But the days of Christendom are over, even if the habits of thought persist. What is striking about the church in the United States is how often recent attempts to revitalize it continue to presuppose the Christendom model. For example, in church marketing (as even the name suggests), the church building and its institutional structure are still at the heart of this new model. The issue for church marketers is not: "What would it mean to *be* the church in an age when people no longer have culturally induced reasons for being *in* church." Instead, they ask: "How do we attract people *to* church once our culture makes the church (still understood as a building) seem like a very strange place to be?" All that seems to have changed is that the church building has been transformed from primarily a worship center to a service center. (Consider the changes in architecture over the past half century.) But this shift is only an attempt to dilute the strangeness of the church.

In short, the serious hearing that church marketing is getting reflects how thoroughly "worldly" the church has become. This points up one of the deep ironies of church marketing: Although it purports to be acting in the name of change and risk, church marketing actually reinforces some of the most powerful and deeply entrenched societal habits of thought and action. In other words, contrary to the advocates of church marketing, the market-driven church is first and foremost the status quo church.

We hasten to add that we are not claiming that market-driven churches (or their advocates) *created* these distorted images of the church described above. They merely embody and extend certain widely accepted habits of thought and action that we think impede the church's attempts to be faithful to its calling. This is a crucial point, because it suggests that church marketing is not first of all a *cause* of the church's confusion about itself, but rather a powerful testi-

mony to and embodiment of that confusion. Said another
way, the church in the United States would not be transformed into a faithful community of Christ if church marketing were suddenly to cease tomorrow.

This is true because the church in the United States has
largely forgotten what it means to be the church. We
believe that the church is called to be a sign, a foretaste, and
a herald of God's present but still emerging kingdom.
Because the hallmark of that kingdom is God's reconciling
work in the world, the church lives to point to, to embody,
and to proclaim that reconciling work. But because this
present-but-still-coming kingdom is a certain kind of kingdom, the church is called to be a certain kind of people. Not
just any kind of community will do. If the convictions that
animate the life of the church are at cross purposes with the
convictions at the heart of this coming kingdom, then the
church will fail to be what God has called it to be. If the
church's embodied life and witness are to be a sign, a foretaste, and a herald of this kingdom, then the church must
strive diligently to embody faithfully those convictions that
make visible this kingdom.

To be this kind of community, the church must embody a
different set of convictions from those that animate most of
the wider society. But as Barna rightly notes, Christians
seem unwilling to do this, and the world around us notices:

> To the average nonbeliever, Christians act no differently
> than anyone else. Our faith appears to be simply a theoreti-
> cal construct, an emotional decision that does not have the
> power to transform who we are and how we behave. During
> the '90s, we must forcefully demonstrate, through our
> actions, that what we believe dictates what we do.[8]

We couldn't agree more. But, as we hope to show in the following pages, we think this forceful demonstration of

Christian living will include leaving behind certain widely accepted techniques for managing the church—including church marketing—that are rooted in convictions at cross purposes with the church's call to be a sign, a foretaste, and a herald of God's reconciling work.

This book is an exercise in what is sometimes called "practical theology." Titles in this genre are often accused of being long on practicality and short on theology. Although this is sometimes true, we do not think such a characterization really gets at the problem. We think it more accurate to say that much "practical theology" seems to ignore the implied (and often problematic) theologies that underwrite and inform many of their recommended techniques and approaches. As such, the following pages are not meant merely for those church people who are wrestling with whether they should be employing marketing strategies and techniques in their churches. They are meant for anyone who suspects both that the twelve images of the church listed above are distorted ones and that there are myriad practices (of which church marketing is only one) that continue to foster these distorted images.

We firmly believe that all theology, when done well, is practical theology. All good theology aids the church in living out its calling in concrete, specifiable ways. By reflecting on the church's practices and convictions (both stated and assumed), we hope to encourage congregations to engage in the crucial process of discerning whether and to what extent they are being faithful to God's calling in Jesus Christ. To do this requires comparing who God has called the church to be with who the contemporary people of God understand themselves to be. This work is never easy, and it is often painful. But it is a task that the church has always thought necessary, lest it awake one day, after years of seemingly inconsequential accommodations, to find itself a frog, boiling in the proverbial kettle.

CHAPTER TWO

Dying for Change

ONE OF THE PARADOXES OF HUMAN LIFE is that change is a constant. Whether we like it or not, change is a part of what it means to be a human being. To their credit, church marketers understand this well, as do those Christians who are enchanted by the marketing approach. Church marketers are right that a church that finds itself increasingly impotent in a rapidly changing environment can ill afford to stand idly by. They rightly understand that the contemporary church in the United States is in deep trouble and that radical changes are necessary if the church is to be revitalized. On this point, we completely agree with church-marketing advocates. Change is not only inevitable, but also necessary, particularly if the church is to regain an intelligible witness to the wider society. So change, by itself, is not the issue.

But changes never happen willy-nilly, nor do they take place in a cultural vacuum. As a result, changes are never changes in the abstract, but changes of a particular kind that lead us in some particular direction. Hence, our arguments with advocates of church marketing are not about change per se (whatever that would be), but about the *kinds* of changes that are being proposed and enacted and the subsequent *direction* in which those changes are leading the church. A great deal more attention and reflection should be focused on these changes and the ways in which they are reshaping the contemporary church. Without some form of theological reflection on these changes, there is no way to discern whether these changes are leading the church in faithful directions.

We wished that our arguments with advocates of church marketing revolved around different (but discussible) theological discernments about whether the market-driven church is headed in the right direction. But most advocates of church marketing shy away from making such discernments. Their silence results from a certain way of thinking about marketing itself. Church marketers assume that marketing is a neutral process or technique that leaves the substance of the faith untouched. Said another way, church marketers believe that marketing affects only the *form* in which the faith is presented, not the *content* of the faith itself. This assumption about the neutrality of marketing takes the church marketers off the theological hook.

This chapter aims to put the church marketers back on the hook. By showing that form and content cannot be divided so neatly, we argue that church marketers cannot dodge questions about the faithfulness of the market-driven church. By doing so, we hope to encourage the advocates of church marketing to discuss these matters in the future rather than sidestepping them by appealing to misleading notions of neutrality.

The Ostensible Neutrality of Church Marketing

Most books about church marketing attempt to address some of the objections that church people have to adopting such techniques. Usually church marketers insist that the problems are primarily matters of semantics: People have hang-ups with "marketing" because they mistakenly equate it with manipulating people to buy things they don't need. While marketing certainly involves selling, advertising, and public relations, these are only a part of the marketing enterprise and are not its distinctive focus. In fact, marketing is best understood, its advocates insist, when we consider it not so much as a technique as an entire way of thinking.

This way of thinking focuses on the managing of exchanges to the benefit of all parties involved. For example, Stevens and Loudon write:

> In our definition of marketing, exchange is the central element. Two or more parties enter into an exchange for the mutual benefit of both parties. Each party has something of value to the other party and both parties are better off after the exchange than they were before the exchange took place. One party, a church or ministry, is offering something needed by the other party [identified in an accompanying diagram as teaching, preaching, guidance, prayers, and fellowship]. The other party, constituents, enters into the exchange and has its needs met while at the same time meeting the needs of the church or ministry [by providing attendance, prayers, services, contributions, and leadership].
>
> A marketer is someone who has the knowledge and skills to understand, plan and manage exchanges. The marketer knows how to go about assessing constituents' needs, developing programs to meet these needs, and then effectively communicating what is offered to the constituents.[1]

There are sound theological reasons for not wanting the church to conceive of itself and its mission in terms of facilitating exchanges. How do church marketers respond when Christians object to this way of thinking, not in general or in principle, but as a way of thinking that is good for the church? What do church marketers say when it is suggested that church marketing may corrupt the church's self-understanding?

27

When such questions are raised, questions that suggest the non-neutral, even distorting, character of church marketing, its advocates attempt to calm our fears. They suggest that our discomfort is rooted in our failure to understand the instrumental character of marketing: Marketing is a neutral tool or technique that need not transform either the content of the gospel or the self-understanding of the church. One group of church marketers writes:

> Metaphorically, a lack of understanding as to the true nature of marketing can be likened to the individual who has seen a hammer being used only as a tool of *destruction* and who, upon being handed a hammer when asking for a tool to use in *construction*, wonders if the other person has taken leave of his senses. In the same way, if marketing has been perceived as only deceptive advertising by dishonest salespersons and as efforts to manipulate demand (tool of destruction), it will be dismissed by individuals or religious institutions when faced with problems that it might help them solve. It is necessary, therefore, to distinguish marketing as a process (facilitating exchange of values) from the sometimes objectionable *use* of that process. . . . When viewed as an exchange-facilitating mechanism, rather than viewing the worst manifestations of its implementation, there is nothing inherent in marketing that would desacralize religion.[2]

We don't know if there is inherent in marketing anything that desacralizes religion; our point is much more concrete than that. We are suggesting that the convictions that animate and structure the marketing enterprise are at cross purposes with the convictions that ought to animate and structure those communities of disciples who place themselves under the lordship of Jesus Christ. Because a congregation's self-understanding is largely shaped by its shared convictions, it should be of enormous concern if those convictions are at odds with who God calls us to be as the church. To see why this is the case, we need to examine some of the assumptions of church marketers.

Empty Forms and Shapeless Contents?

Much of the writing on church marketing assumes that a neat distinction can be made between form and content. For example, Lyle Schaller asks: "Are your leaders willing to change the shape of the vessel that carries the Good News that Jesus Christ is Lord and Savior?"[3] The distinction seems clear. On one side is the unchanging, life-altering substance of the gospel, while on the other are the always changing, flexible ways in which that gospel is communicated to a particular people at a particular time and place. Within such a scheme, marketing is understood as a neutral tool or means for either communicating an unchanging substance or accomplishing a fixed objective. As one group of marketing advocates writes:

> We believe that no organization or group has a message of such urgent and life-changing *content* as the message of faith in God. Yet most churches fail to use the *concepts and tools* which can enable them to effectively communicate to current and prospective members and donors, as well as other groups which need so desperately to hear this message.[4]

For the most part there seems to be little worry that certain strategies or tactics for marketing the church (forms) might adversely affect the character of the gospel or the self-understanding of the community of believers (content). Occasionally a church marketer will whisper a faint warning about the possibility of such corruptions, but this is usually drowned out by loud and repeated insistencies that, although good marketing requires that we alter the packaging (form) of our product, such alterations should and can be made in ways that leave unaffected the content of that product. For example, when George Barna takes up this subject, he assures his readers that church marketing is different from secular marketing because the church is not at liberty to alter the product.

> Unlike a secular organization, in which the product would be manufactured in accordance with the market assessment, the product of the Church has to remain constant. We cannot tinker with our product—how we describe the product, package it, and convey it to our target audience, yes—but the product itself is, so to speak, sacred. . . . Thus, while the Church does not have to worry about conceiving, shaping, producing, and revising a new product, we would do well to remind ourselves exactly what our product is and take every precaution to be certain that we are not in any way, shape, or form changing the product to suit our environment.[5]

Barna does not offer any guidance about how to discern whether the church *has* changed its product to suit its environment; instead, he simply insists that the church should not do so. When Barna acknowledges that church marketing has led certain churches to compromise their identity, he insists that the complete blame for this falls on the users; such examples tell us nothing at all about the instrumental character of church marketing.

> Certainly, there are examples of large, fast-growing churches that soft-sell the gospel, or add elements of their own theology to make the faith more appealing. But the problem in these situations is not that attention to people's needs and trying to market a church is wrong, but that the people entrusted with the responsibility of leading God's people and presenting Him to an inquiring world have chosen to compromise what they believe or how they behave. In other words, the problem is the technician, not the technique.[6]

We will come back to this claim later, but here we want to acknowledge that while there is some truth to such a claim, we think it ultimately rings hollow. Indeed, we tend to think the claim remarkably similar to the National Rifle Association's insistence that "guns don't kill people; people do." At a trivial level, this is no doubt true. But the question critics keep posing to the NRA is whether people find it easier to kill each other unnecessarily when they are carrying a handgun. These critics admit that many people believe there are legitimate uses for certain kinds of guns in certain kinds of settings. The critics could also probably agree with the NRA that most killings would not happen if people were not involved, and even that some killings would still take place regardless of whether a gun was available. But a question remains: Does encouraging people to carry guns facilitate needless killing in ways that are more subtle than the NRA slogan suggests?

Our questions to the church marketers are similar. We realize that there are likely legitimate uses of marketing in the business world. And we realize that people are the ones who ultimately compromise a church's mission and identity when they use church marketing in certain ways. Moreover, we also realize that such compromises can and do happen apart from church marketing. But this does not address the important question: Does encouraging churches to adopt a marketing orientation *facilitate* compromise in ways that are more subtle than Barna's slogan suggests? We believe that it does, and not the least because church marketers insist that their techniques pose no problems for the church, since they are neutral with respect to the content of the church's message.

But this is not all. Because church marketers assume that marketing is neutral, they also conveniently sidestep any discussion about whether using marketing as a means is appropriate to the church's goals or ends. If the means are

31

neutral, then there can be no worry about compatibility. Such compatibility questions only arise after one acknowledges that the convictions underwriting a certain means are never neutral and so may be at odds with a certain end or goal.

What's Wrong with This Picture?

What church marketers seem to deny is something that most of us know from experience: that "forms" always bring with them a certain "content" and that "means" always shape "ends." Perhaps a couple of examples will be instructive.

The American Bible Society (ABS) is currently involved in a multimedia translation program. Part of the impetus for this initiative is the desire to reach people in our society who "are increasingly relying on forms other than print for information and education" (ABS flyer). This initiative involves translating certain portions of Scripture into music videos, which are incorporated into an interactive computer program using CD-ROM technology. One of us routinely uses an ABS music video (based on the story of the prodigal son) in the classroom. First, a couple of representative rock music videos are shown without commentary, and then the ABS video is introduced by briefly noting that many people believe that the music video "form" can be used for good as well as for corrupting purposes. After all three videos have been viewed, the students discuss the similarities and differences among them as well as their respective power and effectiveness as communication tools. These discussions are always interesting and now (after several uses) somewhat predictable, though at first we were a little surprised. Our informal polling suggests that many adults (including the two of us and several other faculty members) who are not immersed in the world of music videos find the ABS video quite powerful and moving, while many younger people tend to view the ABS video as they do other music videos—as primarily entertainment. The irony, of course, is that the very people the ABS most hopes to reach with these videos seem to be those least likely to respond to them on the level the ABS desires. What the ABS seems to be forgetting is that music videos, like any form, are always viewed through a set of cultural expectations that affects whatever the content may be. In short, form and content cannot be neatly separated.

Other everyday examples could be offered to support such a claim. Good teachers (as well as good students) know that *what* is taught (content) cannot easily be separated from *how* something is taught (form). Similarly, most parents can think of child-rearing experiences when they were reminded that what is taught and how it is taught are inseparable. For example, while yelling at children for having raised their voices might be effective in the short run, it is likely that those children will be confused in the long run by the mixed signals.

The Non-Neutrality of Church Marketing

Contrary to what the church marketers say, the enterprise of marketing is not a neutral tool, form, or means to advance any end or to communicate any content. Rather, marketing is a value-laden enterprise rooted in specific sets of convictions. Our argument is not whether the process of marketing can be used in ways that certain people might judge helpful or unhelpful; this, indeed, might be the case. But just because something can be used for any number of different purposes does not thereby make it neutral or value free. To take up the example above, cited by the church marketers: Simply because a hammer can be used both for construction and destruction does not mean that a hammer is value neutral. Indeed, having a hammer in one's hand often changes the way one looks at the world: In our experience, holding a hammer in your hand increases the likelihood that you will see everything as a nail. Similarly, having management techniques at one's disposal encourages one to see all people as objects to be managed and controlled, just as having marketing techniques at the center of the picture encourages one to view the entire world as a series of manageable exchanges.

We are not trying to paint marketing as an evil enterprise. Neither are we arguing that Christians who engage in marketing practices are somehow sub-Christian. Instead, we believe that it is a serious mistake to place at the center of the church's self-understanding what the church marketers so innocuously call a "marketing orientation." If during the week you work for the marketing department of Proctor & Gamble, that may or may not be a problem for you as a Christian (that's the subject for another book). We question the appropriateness of placing an entirely new way of thinking—a self-conscious marketing orientation—at the center of a congregation's self-understanding. And the reason why we question this is that the convictions that are at marketing's heart don't seem to be those at the heart of the gospel, but those at the core of modern marketing and management philosophies. As a result, marketing threatens to refashion the church in its own image. Or, to use the language of which church marketers are fond, church marketing does indeed change the "product" of the church, their protestations to the contrary notwithstanding.

The remaining chapters of this book examine church marketing's central concepts and practices. Each chapter explains why marketers believe that these concepts or practices are central to their unique approach. Each chapter also examines the underlying (and often unarticulated) convictions that animate these concepts and practices. Finally, in each chapter we attempt to explain why asking the church to adopt these sets of convictions and practices places the church at odds with a number of convictions that Christians throughout the ages have believed are central to its self-understanding. In short, we believe that adopting a marketing orientation runs the risk of transforming the church into a kind of community God never desired it to be. Perhaps more important, we believe that adopting a marketing orientation makes it less likely that the church will be able to fulfill its calling to be a sign, a foretaste, and a herald of God's new creation.

Dying for Change

It has been said that the church is dying for change.[7] We believe this is true, though not necessarily for the reasons that church marketers have thought. No doubt there are congregations out there who dig in their heels in order to avoid change. These churches certainly ought to be encouraged to think differently about the dynamics of change. Nevertheless, these churches are not our main concern here. We are most concerned about those congregations who eagerly adopt the latest techniques for helping their churches to grow by making them more "responsive" without pausing to consider fully the theological ramifications of such practices. We hope that our brothers and sisters in Christ will carefully consider the ways in which marketing practices are rooted in convictions that are at odds with the convictions Christians are called to embody as Christ's church.

CHAPTER THREE

Marketing the Church

Marketing the Church Marketing the Chur

REFLECTING THEOLOGICALLY ON church marketing requires that we do our best to understand what distinguishes the practice of marketing from other activities. Once we understand that marketing is not a neutral technique, but an activity already embedded within a set of convictions, practices, and narratives that makes this activity intelligible, we see the importance of probing the history of this practice. If one wanted to understand what makes baseball the peculiar pastime that it is in American society, one would have to do more than simply read the rule book. One would also have to examine the convictions that it embodies (that one game shouldn't make or break a season), the corollary practices that inform and shape it (the detailed keeping of statistics, including errors), and the narratives that become inextricable from and metaphors for our common life (the Black Sox scandal of 1919 or the Iron Man legacy of Cal Ripkin, Jr.). In the same way, marketing stands within a certain tradition—a certain historical way of thinking about the world and our place within it—that we must examine if we are to understand what differentiates marketing from other activities.

What Makes Marketing Different?

Many marketing textbooks begin by offering a definition of *marketing*, such as the one articulated by the American Marketing Association in 1985: "Marketing is the process of planning and executing the conception, pricing, promotion, and distribution of ideas, goods and services to create exchanges that will satisfy individual and organizational objectives."[1] As useful as such a definition might be in narrowing our focus, it offers little help in determining what differentiates marketing from other approaches. To do that, we need not merely a definition, but also a story, and this is precisely what the marketers offer.

This story traces the increasingly central role that marketing has played in highly specialized economies, such as those found in North America and Western Europe. This drama has three acts, or three successive eras: the production era, the sales era, and the marketing era.[2] The production era, which lasted until the 1920s, was rooted in the conviction that a good product will sell itself. Businesses during this era focused primarily on making quality products and then only later looking for people to buy them. Robert J. Keith, the former CEO of Pillsbury, wrote an influential article in 1962 in which he recounted how his company moved through these three successive stages, finally coming to embrace the "marketing revolution." Here's how he described his company during the "production era":

> We are professional flour millers. Blessed with a supply of the finest North American wheat, plenty of water power, and excellent milling machinery, we produce flour of the highest quality. Our basic function is to mill high-quality flour, and, of course (and almost incidentally), we must hire salesmen to sell it, just as we hire accountants to keep our books.[3]

An orientation to production made sense during the early years of industrialization, when production shortages were common and consumer demand remained high. This orientation largely accounts for Henry Ford's seemingly cavalier attitude toward his customers, whom he assured could have his cars in "any color they want, as long as it's black."[4]

A transition from a production orientation to a sales orientation took place during the second quarter of this century (1925–1950). This shift was deemed necessary because of two societal changes. First, with the development of more sophisticated production techniques, output was at an all-time high (though much of this output would soon be diverted to the war effort). Hence, finding customers for new products became more important than ever. But second, and equally important, in the shadow of the Great Depression and World War I (and later in the midst of World War II), customers often hesitated to buy more than the necessities. Thus aggressive sales forces and advertising took on new importance. Here's how Keith described Pillsbury during the "sales era":

> We are a flour-milling company, manufacturing a number of products for the consumer market. We must have a first-rate sales organization which can dispose of all the products we can make at a favorable price. We must back up this sales force with consumer advertising and market intelligence. We want our sales representatives and our dealers to have all the tools they need for moving the output of our plants to the consumer.[5]

The "marketing era" emerged after World War II. The primary driving force behind this transformation was the shift from a seller's market (where there is a shortage of goods and services) to a buyer's market (where there is an abundance of goods and services). In other words, once the extraordinary manufacturing capacity of the United States was directed away from the war effort to the production of consumer goods, American consumers found themselves inundated with new and competing products. This surplus of consumer goods gave the consumer unprecedented power in the marketplace. Businesses that wanted to survive in this increasingly competitive environment had little choice but to acknowledge that "the customer was king." As a result, the new motto of business became "find a need and fill it." This new consumer orientation radically changed the management philosophy of most businesses. Here's how Keith described the "marketing revolution" that was then taking place at Pillsbury:

> [At Pillsbury] marketing will become the basic motivating force for the entire corporation. Soon it will be true that every activity of the corporation—from finance to sales to promotion—is aimed at satisfying the needs and desires of the consumer. When that stage is reached, the marketing revolution will be complete.[6]

Is there any doubt about the pervasiveness of this marketing revolution? It would be a grave mistake to assume that this revolution has affected only the business side; consumers are more aware than ever of the enormous power they wield. This revolution has created an entirely new way of thinking—a way of thinking rooted in the conviction that other people ought to be prepared to satisfy our desires. Thus friendships and marriages increasingly reflect this consumer orientation, with their easy dissolution often viewed on a par with changing brands. College and university faculties often find themselves torn between teaching what they think students need to know and what students (as consumers) want to be taught. The "news industry" struggles to resist defining what is "newsworthy" by what attracts the largest number of viewers or readers. Is there any area of life that has remained untouched by this new consumer orientation?

If most of our lives are indeed shaped by this consumer orientation, should we really be surprised if we find this way of thinking not only present in the church, but also encouraged there? Why should the church be exempt from the logic of the marketplace? Certainly the disestablishment of religion in the United States created competition, and hence a buyer's market, from the very beginning.[7] Yet we may still ask whether on balance this development has been good for the church, and if not, what might be done about it.

We continue to hope that people will recognize the wisdom of placing some things outside the logic of the marketplace. For example, Great Britain forbids the buying and selling of blood and blood products, believing that living human tissues should not be regarded as marketable commodities. Even in the United States, where blood and blood products are routinely bought and sold, and where the Federal Trade Commission has ruled that human blood is a commodity, most people remain uncomfortable with the idea of marketing human body parts.[8] Although it is difficult to predict whether the American public will continue to view with horror the prospect of organ harvesting and marketing, we are glad that such a consensus presently exists. Might there also be wisdom in attempting to keep the Body of Christ from being marketed?

Are Church Marketers Marketing or Selling Marketing?

If we want additional insight into the peculiar character of marketing, a most illuminating exercise is to examine how church marketers themselves market their product (marketing). Imagine that you are a marketer faced with the following difficult assignment: You must *market the process of marketing* to the church, an audience that is guaranteed to have serious reservations about adopting such an innovation. What do you do?

One approach would be to do two very different, even contradictory things—at the same time. First, you try to convince the audience that they do, indeed, need what you're offering, that marketing offers them a new, state-of-the-art, cutting-edge solution to their problems. By playing on the "up-to-dateness" as well as the "acceptability" of the marketing approach among successful (profitable) businesses, you play on the desire of most modern people to be associated with cutting-edge, successful enterprises.

But you must also sound a different note, a note directed at disarming some of the reservations that this particular audience has about incorporating innovations into the church. Here the strategy is quite different. Rather than emphasizing the novelty of marketing, you attempt to convince your audience that marketing is not an innovation at all. You insist repeatedly that their church is already engaged in marketing, whether they call it that or not (so how dangerous can it be?), and that, in fact, Jesus was himself a master marketer and that the Bible is itself "one of the world's great marketing texts."[9] Who can possibly object to such an innovation if it turns out that it's not an innovation at all, but the very approach that Jesus Christ himself used and of which the Bible is one of the supreme exemplars?

This sometimes confusing, yet clever, approach is exactly the one taken by most of the advocates of church marketing. First, listen as the church marketers assure us that the church needs to adopt this new marketing perspective if it is to be successful and effective, and that most churches are currently failing miserably at the marketing enterprise:

To immediately expect pastors and other church leaders to *blast forward* with *cutting-edge* ministry strategies and tactics,

41

based upon a *newly-embraced,* marketing-driven mind-set may have been expecting too much.[10]

Basically, the book presents a *new way* of conceptualizing, planning, and implementing ministry.[11]

The Christian Church in America, with a few exceptions, *does not have a marketing perspective* regarding its growth and development. Marketing by default—that is, letting events determine the way in which a product or service is shaped, priced, promoted, and disseminated—inevitably leads to *failure by neglect.* Sadly, research studies have shown that marketing, as a conscious set of activities growing out of an articulated marketing philosophy, is absent in more than nine out of ten evangelical churches. Most churches, by marketing standards, are *failures*: that is, they are not maximizing their potential for profit (i.e., ministry gains).[12]

My contention, based on careful study of data and the activities of American churches, is that the major problem plaguing the Church is its *failure* to embrace a marketing orientation in what has become a market-driven environment.[13]

Second, listen as the church marketers try to calm our fears about marketing the church by insisting that we're already doing it, even if we don't call it that, and that the Bible is full of examples of good marketing:

The fight over whether to market is false. *Every church markets.* When a church puts its name on a building or prints up a bulletin for Sunday services or prints business cards for the pastor, it markets.[14]

Think about your experience for a minute. When you share your faith with a nonbeliever, you are actually marketing the church. When you place an advertisement in the newspaper to inform people of your church services, you are marketing your church. If your church has a sign on the church grounds, identifying the times of services, Sunday school classes, or even the title of the upcoming sermon, you are engaged in marketing. Every time your pastor accepts an invitation to offer a benediction at a public gathering (although he has been invited for the purpose of ministry), his presence and performance represent an exercise in marketing.[15]

As we shall see in the following chapters, the Bible is replete with examples of the use of marketing techniques by individuals pursuing honorable ends.[16]

We could spend more time dissecting the Bible to see exactly how the Lord Jesus, the apostles, the prophets, and others in leadership positions utilized basic marketing techniques to further God's Kingdom. However, the point is indisputable: the Bible does not warn against the evils of marketing. In fact, the Scriptures provide clear examples of God's chosen men using those principles. So it behooves us to not waste time bickering about techniques and processes, but to study methods by which we can glorify our King and comply with the Great Commission.[17]

It's curious how church marketers seem to want to have it both ways. On the one hand, what they are doing is new and different, and they want to persuade you that your church would benefit if it would only be willing to try this new approach. But on the other hand, what the church marketers are asking you to do is what you are supposedly already doing; in fact, Jesus, the apostles, and Paul were all engaged in it as well (even though they didn't call it that), and so any objection to the practice can only be a matter of semantics.

What's going on here? Perhaps church marketers *are* making an important distinction, but not making it very clearly, since to do so would not be in their best interest. The distinction that they occasionally hint at is the one between the component techniques of the process of marketing (such as research, product positioning, awareness development, strategic planning, pricing, advertising, public relations, and audience segmentation)[18] and the systematic process taken as a whole, which they often refer to as a "marketing orientation." When they do make this distinction, it's often to make the point that churches that engage in only one or two of these aren't really engaged in marketing in the true sense.

> Marketing is not selling, advertising, or promotion—though it may include all of these. *Marketing is the analysis, planning, implementation, and control of carefully formulated programs to bring about voluntary "exchanges" with specifically targeted groups for the purpose of achieving the organization's missional objectives.*[19]

A congregation that wants to pursue its mission effectively, therefore, cannot simply be satisfied with doing a little marketing (taking up a few of the techniques), but must adopt a full-blown marketing or consumer orientation. The reason for belaboring this point is that we believe it helps to cut through some of the confusing claims of the church marketers. When church marketers insist that Jesus and the apostles did marketing and that most contemporary churches are already "doing marketing," they are conveniently pointing to a few of the component parts of the marketing process (usually those involving some form of planning and persuasion). What they fail to acknowledge is that Jesus and the apostles did not have a "marketing" or "consumer orientation," which is what they insist the contemporary church must have if it is to be effective. The reason why Jesus and the early church did not have this orientation is quite simple: As we have shown, the management theory that underwrites such an approach to marketing was developed during the middle part of the twentieth century under very historically specific circumstances. As a species of organizational management, marketing in this narrow sense is a relatively young discipline, something that all marketers acknowledge somewhere along the line. One group writes: "As an organized theory, marketing is a new kid on the block, having matured as a science and an art in the last thirty years."[20]

Thus the logic of the marketers' position is something akin to the following. Dave Diet writes a book commending the virtues of his new scientifically informed, systematic weight-loss plan. The plan involves a series of processes and techniques, such as nutrition awareness, abstaining from certain foods (like red meat), routine exercise, goal setting, frequent weighings, and an intricate evaluation and reward system. The novelty of his plan is found not so much in any of these techniques, but in the whole series when employed as a systematic method for losing weight. Some of Dave's detractors note that while Dave's plan does seem to "work" for a lot of people, this is perhaps besides the point. These detractors insist that rather than focusing on the success or failure of Dave's new method, considerable attention needs to be paid to the relatively recent fixation, if not obsession, that many Americans have with controlling their weight. In other words, it's largely because many Americans have a narrow and warped sense of what it means to be physically attractive that any of this is an issue in the first place. Dave responds to these criticisms by insisting that his method isn't really new; in fact, people through the centuries (including his detractors) have employed many of these same techniques. "Think about every time you choose to eat nutritiously or pass up that fat-filled piece of meat," says Dave. "You're really dieting. Or think about every time you exercise or set goals or step on the scales or evaluate or reward yourself—you're already engaged in the activity of dieting. Sure, you may choose to call it something else, and you can continue to do so if that makes you feel more comfortable, but at least be honest enough to admit that what you're doing when you engage in any of these activities is dieting."

Perhaps now one of the fallacies underlying the marketing position becomes clear. Although it would be convenient for Dave to claim for his own cause all people who ever ate nutritiously, abstained from food, exercised, set goals, weighed themselves, and so on, such a move neglects to take into account that these same activities or practices can be ordered to quite different goals and purposes, thus making them quite different practices after all. For example, an anorexic teenager who abstains from eating a hamburger because the fat content will "ruin her figure" is not doing the same thing that a vegetarian is doing when she abstains because she believes killing animals for food is unnecessary and immoral, even though superficially each is abstaining. Similarly, only those already preoccupied with dieting, and who thereby seem to see it everywhere, would think that a monk who was fasting, a runner training for a marathon, or a third-grader who sets herself the goal of reading ten books over the summer is already employing "dieting techniques." Such persons *are* abstaining from food, exercising, or setting goals, but they are doing so for quite different reasons and toward quite different ends. As a result, what they think of systematic dieting is another matter altogether.

Thus when church marketers insist that Jesus and the apostles employed marketing techniques, we should pause and reflect. Church marketers may commend practices that look, at least on the surface, like many of the things that Jesus and the early church did. But the differences should not be passed over lightly. For example, church marketers insist that the "marketing approach requires that the congregation systematically study needs, wants, perceptions, preferences, and satisfaction of its members and others whom it is trying to reach," and then that "the planners must act on this information to meet those needs more effectively."[21] Is this what God has called us to do? Is this what Jesus was doing when he sent out the twelve to proclaim the nearness of the kingdom, instructing them that if anyone would not welcome them or listen to them that they should shake off the dust from their feet on their way out of the house or town (Matt. 10:14; Mark 6:11; Luke 9:5)? Granted, these are not the only examples from Scripture that need to be examined, but they should caution us against too quickly granting that Jesus and the early church had a marketing or consumer orientation.

Our point in taking this brief detour is to show that church marketers have not in any convincing fashion demonstrated that their practice is warranted by Scripture. This, by itself, is no major victory, except that some go to great (and occasionally ridiculous) lengths to convince us that their practice *is* so warranted.[22] Our reason for countering their insistence is straightforward. We intend to raise serious theological objections throughout this book to the practice of marketing the church, and we do not want consideration of these matters to be short-circuited by quick and misleading appeals to biblical precedent.

All the World's an Exchange

Once we see that Scripture does not necessarily warrant marketing the church, we are free to ask hard questions about the marketing model. One of the first important questions concerns conceptual fit: How does employing marketing concepts reshape the church's identity? Viewing the world with a marketing mentality shapes the way we conceive of everything, including the church. There is always the possibility that trying to force the church into a marketing model will do serious harm to the church's self-understanding.

For example, marketers insist that the distinctiveness of their approach is the way in which marketing views everything through the mechanism of exchange. As one marketing textbook states: "The essence of marketing is the exchange process, in which two or more parties give something of value to each other to satisfy felt needs."[23] Again, such a process may be fine for American Airlines, but we should proceed cautiously before assuming that such an approach is in line with the way we should conceive of the church. Does making the exchange process central to the way we tell and embody our story allow us to tell it faithfully? We don't think so. In fact, we think placing exchange at the heart of our story distorts the church and its narrative in several ways.

For example, who exactly is involved in these exchanges? Church marketers claim that at least some of the exchanges are between the individual and God. Yet God does not lack, and so has no need for exchanges. As Paul says, "The God who made the world and everything in it, he who is Lord of heaven and earth, does not live in shrines made by human hands, nor is he served by human hands, as though he needed anything, since he himself gives to all mortals life and breath and all things" (Acts 17:24-25). Hence, our worship of God is service, but it is also gratuitous—God does not "need" it, nor has God entered into an exchange for it. It is our gift that we bring as a response to God's gift. Irenaeus, Bishop of Lyons in the late second century, perhaps best articulated this truth:

> God created Adam in the beginning, not because he needs the human race, but so that he might have a recipient of his

generosity. Moreover, God commanded us to follow Christ, not because he has any need of our service, but because he wants to give us salvation. To follow the saviour is to share in salvation, just as to follow the light is to gain the light. People who are in the light do not themselves provide the light but are illuminated and made bright by it; they do not contribute anything to it but, by being illuminated, they receive the benefit of the light. Similarly, to serve God does not mean giving him any gift, nor has God any need of our service. On the contrary, it is he who gives to those who serve him life, immortality and eternal glory. He rewards those who serve him without deriving any benefit himself from their service: he is rich, he is perfect, he has no needs. God requests human obedience so that his love and his pity may have an opportunity of doing good to those who serve him diligently. The less God has need of anything, the more human beings need to be united with him. Consequently, a human being's true glory is to persevere in the service of God.[24]

Irenaeus reminds us of a crucial point: The concept of gift is critically central to the logic of Christian convictions.[25] But when we view the entire world through the marketing lens, the notion of gift disappears. Should Christians be so willing to give up on the notion of "gift," replacing it instead with the concept of self-interested exchange? We believe that replacing the concept of gift with that of exchange corrupts our relationship with God and our relationships with other people.

Our Relationship with God: A Self-interested Exchange?

Most Christians would want to affirm that our redemption in Christ is God's gift; we have done nothing to merit this gift and can do nothing to repay this "debt." As Paul writes, we are "justified by [God's] grace as a gift, through the redemption that is in Christ Jesus" (Rom. 3:24). And as the writer of the Apocalypse urges, "Let anyone who wishes take the water of life as a gift" (Rev. 22:17). In fact, the beginning of Romans 4 appears to be directed toward those people who think that their works can place God under obligation. As Paul notes, something was gained by Abraham, but what was gained was a gift, not a wage (a form of exchange):

> What then are we to say was gained by Abraham, our ancestor according to the flesh? For if Abraham was justified by works, he has something to boast about, but not before God. For what does the scripture say? "Abraham believed God, and it was reckoned to him as righteousness." Now to one who works, wages are not reckoned as a gift but as something due. But to one who without works trusts him who justifies the ungodly, such faith is reckoned as righteousness. (Rom. 4:1-5; cf. Eph. 2:1-10)

But what about the so-called ransom view of the atonement? Isn't this a form of exchange? While it is true that several prominent theologians of the church have often spoken of a "ransom" view of the atonement, many have also realized that the image has serious limitations. For example, many scholars have puzzled over the question of to whom God paid the ransom. Some believed the answer was that God paid the ransom to evil, to death, or to the devil, but others found this very unsatisfactory. Indeed, some theologians, such as Gregory of Nazianzus, thought these problems so insurmountable that he rejected the ransom theory altogether. But for our purposes, this debate is somewhat besides the point. Even if we grant that God paid a ransom for human beings, no one in the history of the church thought that human beings were actors in this exchange. We are the beneficiaries of God's work of redemption, however we conceptualize it, and we must never allow the prominence of the exchange metaphor to tempt us into believing that we have struck a deal with God.

Often marketers write as if what Christians get in the exchange is eternal life. But Paul has a more complex view of the matter. Eternal life is a gift, and it is the goal or *telos* of the Christian life; it is where we are headed. The advantage Christians gain by being enslaved to God is not eternal life per se, but sanctification—the process of being made a holy people.

> When you were slaves of sin, you were free in regard to righteousness. So what advantage did you then get from the things of which you now are ashamed? The end of those things is death. But now that you have been freed from sin and enslaved to God, the advantage you get is sanctification. The end is eternal life. For the wages of sin is death, but the free gift of God is eternal life in Christ Jesus our Lord. (Rom. 6:20-23)

What Christians have exchanged, then, is one master for another. One master's gift was the gift of death; the other master's gift was the gift of eternal life. We have, by God's grace, been placed in a position to receive God's free gift; we have not exchanged something for it in the economic sense. In Luther's classic image, when we are united with Christ as a bride is with her bridegroom and become one flesh, Christ takes upon himself our sin and death, while conferring on us his righteousness, life, and salvation.[26] We are made holy by God, and thus we are presumably capable of deeper intimacy with God and our fellow Christians. This is why the Christian tradition has insisted that the most precious gift that God gives is God's own presence, God's own self. God is not a means to some other end that we desire. God's presence is its own end, its own reward.

Thus, when Augustine offers instruction about prayer, he writes:

> When you turn to God, do not seek some favour from him. Seek the Lord himself and he will hear you. He will interrupt your prayer saying: "Here I am. Yes, surely, here I am, here. What do you want? What is your request? Everything I can give you is nothing in comparison to the gift of myself. Accept me, find your joy in me, talk with me. Touch me with the hands of your faith and you will be united to me."[27]

Paul also makes it clear that although we might come to Christ or to deeper maturity through the cooperation of human teachers, this does not alter the character of this process as a gift. This is why he rebuked the Corinthians, who had created factions among themselves on the basis of loyalty to their teachers, as if they were responsible. But Paul wrote: "What do you have that you did not receive? And if you received it, why do you boast as if it were not a gift?" (1 Cor. 4:7).

But redemption and sanctification are not the only gifts of which Scripture speaks. For example, the Holy Spirit is often referred to as God's gift. In a telling passage in Acts 8, a man named Simon is rebuked for trying to exchange money for the power to confer the Holy Spirit. Peter says: "May your silver perish with you, because you thought you could obtain God's gift with money!" (Acts 8:20).

Few Christians would stoop to such a perverted view of God's good gifts; yet the pervasiveness of the exchange mentality might tempt us into thinking that we can place God under obligation. For example, if we read the account of Pentecost through the lens of exchange, we might think that Peter is offering his listeners an attractive deal: If they repent and are baptized, they "will receive the gift of the Holy Spirit" (Acts 2:38). The exchange mentality might encourage us to transform God's gift of the Holy Spirit into something that God is obliged to give us in return for our willingness to repent and be baptized. Yet the stories in Acts 8 (of people who have been baptized but have not yet received the Spirit) and Acts 10 (of people who have received the gift of the Spirit but have not yet been baptized) remind us that God remains the sovereign giver of this gift. Indeed, Acts 11:17-18 reminds us that both the Holy Spirit and "the repentance that leads to life" are given by God. We do not place God under obligation by our actions; rather, we respond to God's prior activity.

O the depth of the riches and wisdom and knowledge of God! How unsearchable are his judgments and how inscrutable his ways!
"For who has known the mind of the Lord?
Or who has been his counselor?"
"Or who has given a gift to him,
to receive a gift in return?"
For from him and through him and to him are all things. To him be the glory forever. Amen. (Rom. 11:33-36)

Or as Karl Barth comments on Rom 11:35: "It is impossible to lay hold of [God]. Men cannot bind Him, or put Him under an obligation, or enter into some reciprocal relationship with Him."[28] This is also Peter's emphasis in Acts 2. It is because the Lord our God calls that we are able to respond. In Ephesians, Paul makes a similar point: He is a servant of this gospel as a result of the gift of God's grace (Eph. 3:7). Whatever this relationship is, it is not one of exchange between two self-interested parties looking for a "win-win" solution to their problems. Rather, this relationship is grounded in the always prior action of God, what Reformation theologians have often referred to as God's prevenient grace.

Our Relationships with Others:
A Self-interested Exchange?

Many passages of Scripture suggest that Christians are set apart from the rest of the world because they imitate the character of God. Central to that character, according to Scripture, is that God does not allow the concept of reciprocity to control the way God treats people. When Jesus sends out the twelve, he instructs them to give in the same way in which they have received: "As you go, proclaim the good news, 'The kingdom of heaven has come near.' Cure the sick, raise the dead, cleanse the lepers, cast out demons. You received without payment; give without payment" (Matt. 10:7-8).

In the same way, Christians are called to love those who do not love them in return, because this is how God loves:

> "You have heard that it was said, 'You shall love your neigh-
> bor and hate your enemy.' But I say to you, Love your ene-
> mies and pray for those who persecute you, so that you may
> be children of your Father in heaven; for he makes his sun
> rise on the evil and on the good, and sends rain on the righ-
> teous and on the unrighteous. For if you love those who
> love you, what reward do you have? Do not even the tax col-
> lectors do the same? And if you greet only your brothers and
> sisters, what more are you doing than others? Do not even
> the Gentiles do the same?" (Matt. 5:43-47)

Other passages suggest that even if God's economy can be discussed in the language of exchange, it is an economy that operates on principles much different from those that structure everyday business exchanges. For example, God's economy asks us to trust that someday we will be rewarded; we are not to look for our reward here and now. The author of Colossians, when instructing slaves, wrote: "Whatever your task, put yourselves into it, as done for the Lord and not for your masters, since you know that from the Lord you will receive the inheritance as your reward; you serve the Lord Christ" (3:23-24). Our tendency is to focus on the word *reward*, and assume that this reward is for services rendered, as a form of exchange. But the author makes clear that our reward is an "inheritance." Most of us realize that an inheritance is more like a gift given than a reward earned, since we had little control over who our family was. Similarly, if God has graciously given us new life and adopted us into the household of God, the inheritance that goes with that privilege is not so much our birthright as a freely given gift.

This suggests that God's promised inheritance, whatever it is, must take a back seat to obedience and faithfulness, for we cannot place God under obligation. If the reward is given, it will be given by God in God's own time and in God's own way. Thus as Christians we are freed from the seeming necessity of calculating our own interest at every turn; instead, we are freed to reach out to others with abandon, both to those who can offer little in return and to those who desire to do us harm.

> "When you give a luncheon or a dinner, do not invite your friends or your brothers or your relatives or rich neighbors, in case they may invite you in return, and you would be repaid. But when you give a banquet, invite the poor, the crippled, the lame, and the blind. And you will be blessed, because they cannot repay you, for you will be repaid at the resurrection of the righteous." (Luke 14:12-14)

> Do not repay evil for evil or abuse for abuse; but, on the contrary, repay with a blessing. It is for this that you were called—that you might inherit a blessing. (1 Pet. 3:9)

The exchange theory, especially as it is rooted in self-interested exchanges designed to benefit both parties, also mutes the Scriptures' call to self-denial and self-sacrifice. Here again our model is Jesus, whose example does not fit into the exchange model. When Paul urged the Corinthians to give generously to relieve the saints at Jerusalem, he reminded them of Jesus' sacrifice: "For you know the generous act of our Lord Jesus Christ, that though he was rich, yet for your sakes he became poor, so that by his poverty you might become rich" (2 Cor 8:9). A similar note resounds in the famous Philippian hymn:

> Do nothing from selfish ambition or conceit, but in humility regard others as better than yourselves. Let each of you look not to your own interests, but to the interests of others. Let the same mind be in you that was in Christ Jesus,
> who, though he was in the form of God,
> did not regard equality with God
> as something to be exploited,
> but emptied himself,
> taking the form of a slave,
> being born in human likeness.
> And being found in human form,
> he humbled himself
> and became obedient to the point of death—
> even death on a cross.
>
> Therefore God also highly exalted him
> and gave him the name
> that is above every name,
> so that at the name of Jesus
> every knee should bend,
> in heaven and on earth and under the earth,
> and every tongue should confess
> that Jesus Christ is Lord,
> to the glory of God the Father.
>
> (Phil. 2:3-11)

Both of these passages remind us that the logic of the Christian faith is not the logic of self-interested exchanges. Jesus suffered humiliation, not out of a desire to be exalted, but out of a desire to be obedient. God did in fact exalt him, but it would be mistaken to see that act as the carrot that God dangled in front of Jesus' nose in order to move him to obedience. Rather, Jesus "looks to the interests of others," trusting that such a focus will bring glory not to him, but to God the Father. Here the logic of the Christian faith shows itself as the inversion of Adam Smith's famous "invisible hand" theory of economics. That theory suggested that the most efficient way of meeting needs is for every person to look after his or her own interests. Thus, if people engage in voluntary exchanges with an eye to their own interests, the general welfare of all people will be promoted, even though unintentionally. But the Christian faith has a different assessment of action animated by such self-interest or egoism. Indeed, the Christian tradition often names egoism as the source of most of our sin. For example, Maximus the Confessor, writing in the seventh century, claimed:

> Egoism is the source of the passions. From egoism spring gluttony, avarice, conceit. From gluttony springs lust, from avarice greed, from conceit springs pride. All the other vices, without exception, are merely consequences of this one thing: anger, melancholy, rancour, sloth, envy, slander, and so on. At the beginning of all the passions there is egoism, just as at the end there is pride.[29]

Maximus points us to a deep problem. When a congregation adopts a marketing orientation in order to bring hope and healing to an age marked by deep melancholy, it does little more than fight fire with fire. If Maximus is right, if melancholy does spring largely from egoism, then the church cannot hope to relieve that melancholy by encouraging people to view all their relationships (including that with the church) as a series of self-interested exchanges. Rather, the Christian faith demands a radically different response to egoism. Christians are called to look after the interests of others, trusting both that God has already taken care of our most important needs, and thereby freed us for service, and that God will also take care of any future needs that we might have. Said another way, the exchange mentality locates the church within an economy of need and lack, whereas the economy of salvation in Christ is one of abundance that frees us for service to our neighbor. This freedom from the necessity of securing our own needs and the subsequent freedom for our neighbor has been powerfully articulated by Martin Luther in his *The Freedom of a Christian* (1520):

> We should devote all our works to the welfare of others, since each has such abundant riches in his faith that all his other works and his whole life are a surplus with which he can by voluntary benevolence serve and do good to his neighbor. . . . He ought to think: "Although I am an unworthy and condemned man, my God has given me in Christ all the riches of righteousness and salvation without any merit on my part, out of pure, free mercy, so that from now on I need nothing except faith which believes that this is true. Why should I not therefore freely, joyfully, with all my heart, and with an eager will do all things which I know are pleasing and acceptable to such a Father who has overwhelmed me with his inestimable riches? I will therefore give myself as a Christ to my neighbor, just as Christ offered himself to me; I will do nothing in this life except what I see is necessary, profitable, and salutary to my neighbor, since through faith I have an abundance of all good things in Christ." Behold, from faith thus flow forth love and joy in the Lord, and from love a joyful, willing and free mind that serves one's neighbor willingly and takes no account of gratitude or ingratitude, of praise or blame, gain or loss. For a

man does not serve that he may put men under obligations. He does not distinguish between friends and enemies or anticipate their thankfulness or unthankfulness, but he most freely and most willingly spends himself and all that he has, whether he wastes all on the thankless or whether he gains a reward. . . . Who then can comprehend the riches and the glory of the Christian life? It can do all things and has all things and lacks nothing. It is lord over sin, death, and hell, and yet at the same time it serves, ministers to, and benefits all men. But alas in our day this life is unknown throughout the world; it is neither preached about nor sought after; we are altogether ignorant of our own name and do not know why we are Christians or bear the name of Christians. Surely we are named after Christ, not because he is absent from us, but because he dwells in us, that is, because we believe in him and are Christs one to another and do to our neighbors as Christ does to us.[30]

The Evaporation of Grace and Gift

In short, by making self-interested exchanges central to the church's identity, a marketing orientation corrupts the church's embodied witness to the mercy and grace of the triune God. God's grace is given freely; it is not an exchange. Those who would worship and follow this God are likewise called to live lives that reflect this grace. Those who by God's grace attempt to live such lives already find it incredibly difficult to do so, but the difficulty is only compounded when they are encouraged to view the Christian life as one more example of "I'll scratch your back if you scratch mine"—a mentality that lies at the heart of the marketing enterprise.

Our critique of the central place of self-interested exchange in the marketing enterprise should not, however, be considered a blanket indictment of reciprocity in relationships. After all, people have long regarded reciprocity as vital to human relationships. But there are different kinds of reciprocity. For example, the reciprocity embodied in self-interested exchanges is not the same as the reciprocity embodied in gift giving. As Thomas Murray rightly notes:

> Gifts create moral relationships that are more open-ended, less specifiable, and less contained than contracts. Contracts are well-suited to the marketplace where a strictly limited relationship for a narrow purpose—trading goods and services—is desired. Gifts are better for initiating and sustaining more rounded human relationships, where future expectations are unknown, and where the exchange of goods is secondary in importance to the relationship itself.[31]

In short, gift giving establishes and sustains relationships by acknowledging indebtedness. Thus if you are invited over for dinner this evening at a friend's house, most people would rightly think it inappropriate for you to end the evening's gathering by inviting your friend over for dinner tomorrow night. This too-anxious attempt to avoid indebtedness betrays a lack of trust in the relationship. Being in relationship means being willing to become indebted to others. But this is precisely the kind of indebtedness that self-interested market exchanges seek to avoid. When you walk out of a grocery store after having plopped down $3.79 for a box of cereal, you don't feel indebted to anyone. You gave the grocery store what it wanted, and it gave you what you wanted. You are, as we like to say, "even." And because this is a completely impersonal and abstract exchange, no relationship is established or sustained.[32] You and the check-out clerk, for all practical purposes, remain strangers.

Sociologist Max Weber, early in this century, saw the dangers of making such impersonal exchanges the central feature of corporate life:

The market community, as such, is the most impersonal relationship of practical life into which human beings can enter with one another. Where the market is allowed to follow its own tendencies, its participants do not look toward the person of each other, but only toward the commodity. There are no obligations of brotherliness or reverence, and none of those spontaneous human relations that are sustained by personal unions. They all would just obstruct the free development of the bare market relationship. Such absolute depersonalization is contrary to all elementary forms of human relations.[33]

Perhaps some of the deep incompatibilities between the "logic" of marketing and the "logic" of Christianity are now becoming apparent. If the very character of marketing relationships is impersonal and dehumanizing, does it make sense for the church to adopt a marketing orientation in the name of Christian ministry? Is it wise, for example, to encourage people to think of evangelism as an exercise in brokering self-interested exchanges? Barna, in summarizing the ways in which an evangelistic encounter is actually an exchange, writes:

You, the believer, are the middleman; the Holy Spirit is the other party invisible to, but necessary for, the closure of the deal.

Marketing works well when the objective of both parties is fairness and mutual satisfaction. Fairness means that the exchange is completed with full disclosure by both parties, and that both parties are pursuing a reasonable deal. Mutual satisfaction is generally achieved by attempting to understand and fulfill the needs of the other party, while seeking some response from the party that will fulfill your needs.

Ministry, in essence, has the same objective as marketing: to meet people's needs. Christian ministry, by definition, meets people's real needs by providing them with biblical solutions to their life circumstances.[34]

In contrast, Karl Barth, writing years before Barna, when "selling" was more prominent than "marketing," cautioned those who would reduce the Christian life to an exchange:

> The word of God is not for sale; and therefore it has no need of shrewd salesmen. The word of God is not seeking patrons; therefore it refuses price cutting and bargaining; therefore it has no need of middlemen. The word of God does not compete with other commodities which are being offered to men on the bargain counter of life. It does not care to be sold at any price. It only desires to be its own genuine self, without being compelled to suffer alterations and modifications. . . . It will, however, not stoop to overcome resistance with bargain counter methods. Promoters' successes are sham victories; their crowded churches and the breathlessness of their audiences have nothing in common with the word of God.[35]

We believe that placing a marketing orientation at the center of the church's life radically alters the shape and character of the Christian faith by redefining the character and mission of the church in terms of manageable exchanges between producers and consumers. Much that is central to the Christian life will not fit neatly into the management/marketing scheme, and, not surprisingly, these matters are neglected in a marketing paradigm. In effect, the "good news" has been filtered through a rather fine marketing sieve, the result being that many of the less marketable claims that God has on our lives have been removed, leaving for the consumer those aspects of the Christian faith most readily translated into terms of self-interest. This willingness to exploit self-interest as a strategy for benefiting the church is central to the whole marketing orientation, as we will see in the next chapter.

CHAPTER FOUR

User-Friendly Churches

NOT LONG AGO, JIM ENTERED A SUPER-market and ran into Jan Matheny, a woman who only the Sunday before had visited with her husband and three children the church that Jim serves. After exchanging pleasantries, Jim told her how much the church appreciated her visit and how he hoped they would return. Jan replied, "We enjoyed the service, but right now we're just shopping around for the church that meets our needs."

We begin with Jan not because her response is shocking or exceptional, but because she vocalized what countless church shoppers say to themselves and to others every week. In fact, this activity and its accompanying sentiments are so prevalent and accepted that when we have raised critical questions about it with people, most of them have admitted that they couldn't see why anyone would object to such a practice. Over and over again we have been asked, "What's wrong with shopping for the church where I feel most comfortable and where I feel my needs are best met? Doesn't the church exist to meet my needs?"

For many people (including many Christians), this is precisely why the church exists. And, in one sense, the Mathenys of the world are correct: Part of the church's identity and mission is tied to meeting human needs. Certainly the gospel and the central teachings of the church presuppose that human beings are very much in need. For example, God calls us to be reconciled through Jesus Christ, a calling that assumes that we need to be reconciled both to God and to each other. Similarly, when Christians confess that Jesus died for our sins, this confession presupposes that our sinful condition placed us in a position of need, even if we didn't recognize that need.

So the issue is not whether the church should be involved in meeting human needs. Rather, the issue concerns questions that are more difficult to ask, let alone to answer. Which needs should the church attempt to meet? On what basis should this decision be made? Who determines which needs the church will attempt to meet? What authorizes him or her to do so? Does the church's meeting of specific needs serve a larger goal or purpose, or is such activity its own end? Is the church's mission only to meet those needs that people already recognize, or does the "good news" of Jesus Christ also involve learning to name needs differently?

These are not questions often discussed in church-marketing literature. We suspect this is true because the marketing mentality suppresses such questions; on the few occasions when they have surfaced, they are answered from within the marketing framework. To show how this is the case, we examine in some detail two central and closely related marketing concepts: "marketing orientation" and "felt needs."

Constructing the Church Marketing Success Story

We have already noted that church marketers insist that what makes their approach "new" is what they call a "marketing" or "consumer orientation." And we have discussed the way in which they narrate the rise of marketing as a comprehensive approach to business. But what is particularly interesting for our purposes are the ways in which many church marketers narrate the story of contemporary ministry in ways that parallel the history of twentieth-century business practices. For example, one group of church marketers argues that "there are three basic approaches to ministry in American religion today. They are production, sales, and marketing."[1] Where do these models for "ministry" come from? From the history of marketing. As we have seen, most marketing textbooks tell a similar story about the evolution of marketing in the twentieth century.

Within this story that the church marketers construct, the production and selling models of ministry are characterized as being on the side of rigidity, outdatedness, selfishness, and the refusal to acknowledge change, while the marketing approach is the champion of relevance, service, adaptation, vitality, and commitment. For example, note the way in which the so-called production approach to ministry is characterized:

> The production approach to ministry is based on the idea that things aren't changing, that people inside and outside the congregation think and act as they always have. Based on this assumption, it makes sense to "produce" a ministry product that does not change. Since persons and societies do not change all that much, the clergy and congregation can get by well enough by producing an unchanging "product."[2]

By identifying other ministry options with approaches that this narrative has already determined are outdated and superseded, church marketers guarantee that the moral to this story is obvious: If you want to share in the success that contemporary, cutting-edge businesses are enjoying, you need to approach matters the way they do. As long as the options for contemporary ministry are narrated in this fashion, most people will be unable to resist the obvious conclusion that churches need to leave behind their old product- and sales-driven ways and embrace market-driven approaches to ministry.

But it's far from clear that this marketing success story illuminates the ministry options available to the contemporary church. Do churches that perform ministry with non-marketing models really fit so neatly into one of these objectionable alternatives (the production or selling approaches)? Such an identification seems plausible only if we have already determined that the church's ministry is a "product" in search of "consumers." Only then do the options become produce it, sell it, or market it. Consider, for example, the way in which such language shapes the current debate about worship "styles"—debates that are sometimes referred to as "the worship wars."[3] For many churches, these debates are framed by "product" and "consumer" thinking, even if that language is never used. Worship services are viewed as products that congregations offer for consumption, with the primary concern being how to attract and satisfy more customers (or how to keep the ones you've got). Within a discussion framed in this way, market thinking makes perfectly good sense. If worship is a product looking for consumers, then designing a worship service with the consumer's desires as the central concern is likely to be more effective at attracting and retaining those consumers than either the production or the selling model.

But what if a congregation believes its worship is not a product for consumption, but an activity it engages in to the glory and honor of God? Within this framework, "user-friendliness" seems less important. For example, a congregation that believes corporate confession is integral to its worship cannot become preoccupied with whether members or visitors might prefer not being asked to kneel and confess their sins before God. Perhaps the church's leaders need to do a better job of communicating the importance of this practice, but such a congregation cannot with integrity do a survey about whether people "like" confession, and then cater to their suggestion that the church substitute something more "upbeat" or "affirming."[4] Of course, people who themselves view the worship of the church as a product might decide to leave such a church that refused to offer a more appealing product. But simply because there are people in our society who so view the church does not mean that the church must encourage such a view.

This leads us to another problem with the way church marketers frame the discussion about ministry options. Their story often seems to imply that the three options for ministry—production, sales, and marketing—exist in a historical and cultural vacuum and that the advantages of the marketing approach stem primarily from its ability to offer better "service." But occasionally the rest of the story comes out:

> Some congregations have discovered the value of focusing their attention not on production, products, or sales, but on meeting persons' changing needs and interests. They recognize that without satisfied customers, the organizations will soon find themselves customerless and tailspin into oblivion.[5]

What is this "value" that has been discovered by the marketing approach? Put as straightforwardly as we know how, it is that if you treat people like customers, they will act like customers. Or the flip side: When people come expecting to be treated like customers, you will likely benefit if you so treat them. In other words, what the church marketing story fails to emphasize clearly enough is that the engine driving the marketing model is not the congregation that desires a more effective way of "serving," but the consumers of religion who well know that they are in a buyer's market. We have already noted that all marketers acknowledge that the shift from a seller's to a buyer's market is what fueled the move to a marketing approach. But it is also what is fueling the move to a church-marketing approach. By living in a society in which most daily choices are consumer choices, people have come to view their relationship to the church in similar ways. And no doubt churches have done things in the past to encourage them to do so.[6] But once people come to view choosing a church in ways similar to choosing among competing brands and styles of basketball shoes, then enormous pressure is exerted upon the church to conceive of itself in these terms as well. Yet we believe the church does its members (and potential members), as well as the kingdom of God, a terrible disservice when it encourages people to think of the church in marketing terms.

Admittedly, part of what makes the marketing approach so attractive is that it is couched in the language of "service" and "concern for the needs of others," language that does have its place in the logic of Christian faith and practice. But we fear that the marketing approach twists that logic to make it serve the ends of marketing rather than the ends of God's coming kingdom. Contrary to the implications of the marketing success story, the primary issue is not *whether* we will serve but whose ends or purposes we will serve in so doing. For example, church marketers would have us consider our service as one element in a series of self-interested exchanges designed to benefit all parties involved (including ourselves). But should Christians be encouraged to think of their service to others in terms of an exchange? The potential damage to relationships by so doing has perhaps been articulated best by Ferdinand Tönnies in his classic study of different kinds of community. He articulates the kind of relationship established by contracts or self-interested exchanges, where the guiding principle is "I give so that you will give":

What I do for you, I do only as a means to effect your simultaneous, previous or later service for me. Actually and really I want and desire only this. To get something from you is my end; my service is the means thereto, which I naturally contribute unwillingly.[7]

The church has not been called to serve others because we have calculated that we and the church will likely benefit. The church serves others because the people of God are called to be a sign, a foretaste, a herald of a kingdom that is marked by servanthood. Understanding our service in this way does not, of course, preclude God from using our service as a means to further God's kingdom, but it does suggest that whether or how that happens is not something with which the church should be concerned. Moreover, understanding our service in this way reminds us that the service we render must be consonant with our calling as sign, foretaste, and herald of this particular kingdom that Christ has inaugurated. Merely engaging in an activity that people commonly regard as service does not guarantee that we are being faithful to that calling. For example, Peter clearly believed he was serving Jesus in the garden by drawing his sword to protect Jesus. Yet Jesus' stern rebuke suggests that such "service" is no service at all if it embodies convictions that are at cross purposes with his kingdom (Matt. 26:51-53).

One of the deep ironies of the marketing story is the way marketers (whose approach is premised upon human self-interest) cast themselves as the servants of human need while at the same time casting others as great exponents of selfishness. For example, one group of marketers characterizes the distinctiveness of their approach in this way:

Marketing relies on designing the organization's "offering" in terms of the target market's needs and desires, rather than

in terms of the seller's personal tastes. . . . Effective marketing is user-oriented, not seller-oriented.[8]

Similarly, Barna characterizes the product-driven mentality as being motivated by "doing what you desire" in order
to achieve "personal satisfaction," while the market-driven
mentality is motivated by "providing what people need" in
order to achieve "customer satisfaction."[9] Or as Lyle
Schaller draws the distinction, the difference is between
focusing on the needs of the buyer or consumer and focusing on the needs of the seller or producer.[10] Some church
marketers even suggest that their approach is more in tune
with Scripture than are other approaches because theirs
involves "concern for others' needs." They write: "When
properly understood, a marketing orientation can be seen to
adhere to scriptural principles of concern for others' needs
more than the production and selling orientations which
exemplify the approaches taken by many religious organizations in dealing with their 'markets.' "[11]
But surely these ways of characterizing approaches to
ministry that are not market driven do not adequately
reflect what a lot of thoughtful church people believe themselves to be doing when they engage in ministry. Church
marketers assume that ministry is motivated by one of two
things: either what those doing the ministry themselves
want or what those being ministered to need. But what happens in this scheme to what the church believes God
desires?[12] Granted, the church must always guard against
equating its own desires with what God desires. But by suggesting that all non-marketing approaches to ministry are
rooted in selfishness (by being rooted in doing what you
desire instead of in what people say they need), church marketers imply that it is somehow less problematic to equate
what God desires with people's self-determined needs. And
why must our goal be limited to either personal satisfaction

or customer satisfaction? Couldn't we undertake ministries whose goals cannot be adequately characterized in terms of either personal or customer satisfaction? The church is not called to feed the hungry, clothe the naked, or visit the imprisoned because it is seeking personal or customer satisfaction, but because the people of God have been called to bear embodied witness to God's "upside-down" kingdom. Perhaps here we have another example of the way in which language imported from the world of business fails to illuminate the faith and practice of the church.

Hence, the danger of the marketing story is that it too readily (and, we believe, wrongly) assumes that churches should understand themselves as businesses engaged in supplying their customers with certain products and services. If that premise is questioned, then the debate is not simply over whether a church should have a production orientation or a marketing orientation, but more fundamentally over whether a congregation, and those to whom it ministers, should be encouraged to view the church and its faith as one more marketable commodity. We believe that there are churches who want to resist such a view, and we think they are right to do so. But their struggles and perspectives are nowhere acknowledged within this marketing success story; they are simply lumped together with those churches that are "product driven" and that are thereby doomed to fail.

"I Need It If I Say I Do": The Centrality of Felt Needs

We have already suggested that part of the appeal of the marketing approach is that it is clothed in the rhetoric of ministry. Who, after all, could object to the church's being about the business of ministry? But the language of ministry is no less open to distortion and abuse than is any other. The church must press on to inquire about the kind of ministry, the recipients of ministry, and the purposes of ministry.

These questions take us beyond talking about ministry in the abstract and force us to ask hard questions about how the church understands itself and its mission to the world. To their credit, church marketers seem to understand that their approach requires a rethinking of the church's self-understanding and sense of mission. For example, Barna boldly offers the church a completely new paradigm of self-understanding.

> So for the next ten chapters let's suspend any attachments to traditional thinking about church growth. Let's also enter this journey with a common perspective on the local church. *Think of your church not as a religious meeting place, but as a service agency—an entity that exists to satisfy people's needs.* We believe that, in the Person of Jesus Christ and the fellowship of the Body of believers, we have the perfect solution to people's needs. We are well prepared to fulfill those needs—not the needs that we claim people have, but the needs that people themselves recognize and express. Using the same resources the Church already has—time, talent, money, facilities—how can we squeeze the greatest possible results from those resources and achieve our goals as a service agency in the employ of the God of all creation?[13]

Barna no doubt believes that this image of the church's fundamental identity—the church is a service agency that exists to satisfy people's felt needs—is true to the character and mission of the church. We do not. Once the church's fundamental identity has been constructed as a business whose purpose is to serve its constituency by attempting to meet its insatiable and undisciplined desires and needs, all in the name of ministry and furthering the kingdom, then the church is no longer in a position to be what God has called it to be: an embodied witness to the God whom Christians claim to worship. To see why this is the case, we must examine several problematic assumptions that underwrite the "church as service agency" model.

A view of the church's ministry and service that revolves around and is synonymous with meeting felt needs operates with the explicit dogma that all felt needs, by virtue of their being felt, are legitimate. As noted earlier, all church marketers subscribe to this dogma, insisting that the church that has a "market orientation" rather than a "product orientation" will attempt to fulfill "not the needs that we claim people have, but the needs that people themselves recognize and express." Such a view of ministry and service can only corrupt the church, especially when the church lives in the midst of our culture's marketplace of created desires and needs. Advertising is a trillion-dollar industry, a fact that witnesses to its effectiveness in creating needs and desires. Most Americans are deeply formed by this marketplace of created desire, spending vast fortunes in attempts to satisfy those insatiable needs. It would seem that faithfulness to the gospel would call the church to challenge the very ethos of our culture by identifying many of these felt needs as illegitimate. Instead, churches too often cast themselves as one more social institution dedicated to legitimating this marketplace of desire. Such churches, by catering to the whims of discriminating consumers, encourage their constituents to expect the church to function as another service agency whose purpose is to court them by providing a smorgasbord of programs and services. In such cases, "ministry" and "service" underwrite a kingdom other than God's kingdom.

If the church's goal is to meet felt needs, then the danger arises that the entire enterprise will be shaped primarily by those needs that the consumer desires to have satisfied. This consumer orientation in the church echoes the retailing industry's maxim: The customer is always right. Some Christians might legitimately worry that this emphasis on consumer sovereignty might undermine the integrity of the church's witness. But according to one group of marketers, marketing need not lead to accommodation.

> Marketing relies on designing the organization's "offering" in terms of the target market's needs and desires, rather than in terms of the seller's personal tastes. Marketing is a democratic, rather than an elitist, technology. It holds that efforts that try to impose a product on a market are likely to fail if the market perceives that the product, service, or idea is not matched to its needs or wants. . . . Effective marketing is user-oriented, not seller-oriented. This does not imply, however, that one's theology is adjusted to meet a market's demand. It does mean that the process by which a congregation presents its core doctrines, ministries, and programs should be developed by considering the prospective user's perspective, rather than the seller's perspective, of what constitutes value in the offering. Marketing in congregations requires that those in charge put themselves in the "shoes" and mind of the person they want to serve. It requires "outside-in" thinking (the information for planning a ministry comes from the persons the ministry is intended to serve), not "inside-out" thinking (the planners decide they know better what the persons "out there" need). Wrong thinking consists of planning the ministry—and then trying to convince the target group that it really is best for them.[14]

This way of describing the options implies that the central issue in ministry is determining whose view of "value"— the user or the seller—should be the guiding perspective. Yet we remain most bothered by the instrumentalism inherent in this way of putting the matter, which we believe distorts the church's identity and mission. Church marketers, and others who operate with the same instrumentalist assumptions, would refashion the church into a sophisticated and market-sensitive institution whose primary agenda would be establishing its relevance by servicing (and thereby legitimating) people's self-identified needs. Within such a scenario, the focus would no longer be on how the church should form its community and its members as concrete embodiments of the gospel such that it and they continue to offer a profound, perhaps even radical, alternative to the dominant structures and institutions of the day. Instead, the focus would be on, in one church marketer's words, "How—in the midst of a sophisticated, technological, fast-paced, affluent society—you can position your church as a relevant, valuable, and desirable institution for modern man."[15] But on what basis are we to determine the church's relevance, value, and desirability? An emphasis on market orientation and felt needs would insist that something be considered relevant, valuable, and desirable only to the extent that it is deemed such by those consumers we are attempting to engage in exchange.[16] However, such a view is completely antithetical to the message of the gospel. As a result, it is difficult to see how one can "promote" the church in this way without simultaneously disfiguring it.

The marketing mentality imposes on a congregation a certain kind of discipline, though it is not the same discipline that discipleship to Christ entails. The discipline of the marketplace encourages people to view the entire world (including the church) as a venue for self-gratification; in short, the marketing mentality teaches people to inquire incessantly about how any given activity or program meets their always changing list of felt needs. Again, there is simply too much about the life of the church that will not fit this service agency mentality. For example, the heavy emphasis on felt needs all but drowns out the central teaching that the Christian life calls for a radical transformation and reorientation of one's whole way of thinking and behaving. Instead of assuming that membership in the Body of Christ entails far-reaching claims on our lives, church marketers assume that, at least in principle, the church can be made relevant and desirable to almost anyone if we simply know how to market it effectively. But what if one must be given eyes to see the "relevance" of the church? What if the "point" of the church is not accessible by means of human wisdom? If this were true, then any approach that attempted to make the church relevant without challenging people's presuppositions concerning its irrelevance might result in the church's transforming itself into something other than the church of Jesus Christ.

This brings us back to several of the questions with which we started this chapter. Whose needs are we trying to meet, and why have we chosen to meet their needs as opposed to someone else's?[17] Where do these needs come from? Are these felt needs legitimate needs, or have they been artificially created, and do they, though "felt," need to be identified as illegitimate? Is the church's primary mission to meet needs (as the service-agency model suggests), or are there certain kinds of needs of certain kinds of people that we inevitably find ourselves meeting "along the way," so to speak, as a result of our attempts to embody the gospel faithfully?

If church marketers continue to ignore such questions, or to answer them only from within the marketing framework, then it seems likely that they will remain at least partly responsible for transforming the church into one more marketable commodity. For instance, although Barna insists early in his book that churches are not so much in competition with each other as they are with other organizations that demand consumer loyalty, he later introduces a chapter with the story about his family's search for a church "that would be right for us," noting that during their visit to the fourteenth church, "we were struck by the professionalism and the sincerity of what was happening there."[18] Such judgments exemplify the current level of much ecclesial discourse and practice. Judgments about which church to "join" are increasingly made more on the basis of personal preference and taste than they are on any sense of what the church is called to be. Perhaps more accurately, the church is understood more and more as an institution whose goal is to cater to the personal whims and desires of its finicky consumers, keeping them satisfied lest they "take their business elsewhere."

Once one places such a mentality at the center of a church's self-understanding, it seems quite natural to begin formulating the church's mission in such terms. For example, one group of church marketers recommend defining the church's mission in terms of customer groups, customer needs, and alternative technologies:

> A helpful approach to defining mission is to establish the congregation's scope along 3 dimensions. The first is its *customer groups*—namely, *who* is to be served and satisfied. The second is its *customer needs*—namely, what is to be satisfied. The third is *alternative technologies*—namely, *how* persons' needs are to be satisfied.[19]

The authors insist two pages earlier that what Scripture and tradition tell us about our mission must always be "held in tension" with other relevant concerns; however, this part of the mix is never mentioned again. What is mentioned is that a congregation should strive for a mission that is "feasible, distinctive, and motivational." We would like to think that the authors are assuming that the mission will also be faithful to what God has called the church to be. But we worry that these three descriptions of a desirable mission are offered primarily because they derive from and reinforce the marketing mentality; in short, missions such as these will ensure that the church is marketable. Here we have another example of the means reshaping the ends: We must write our mission so that it will allow us to market ourselves effectively. Stated more boldly, we must write our mission so that it serves the ends of marketing, one of which is to confirm people's identity as consumers. That is, we are what we consume. If you doubt that this is what is going on, read the authors' rationale for making distinctiveness a central feature of a mission statement:

> A mission serves best when it is distinctive. A well-stated mission allows persons to make differential comparisons, allowing members and seekers to see how and why this church is different from the other churches in the community, thus helping persons to decide whether this is the church for them. The mission identifies the church's uniqueness, sets it apart from other churches, strengthens its boundaries, and helps members know "who we are." If all churches were carbon copies of one another, there would be little basis for pride in one's particular church. People take pride in belonging to an institution that "does it differently" or "does it better." By cultivating a distinctive mission and personality, an organization stands out more and attracts a more loyal group of members.[20]

By encouraging churches to emphasize distinctiveness, church marketers guarantee that the marketing cycle perpetuates itself. But clearly church marketers are not the only ones operating with such a view of Christian ministry and service. The reason why church marketers are gaining such a wide hearing is not simply because they are offering the church something new, but because they are articulating, formalizing, and systematizing a way of thinking and behaving that is already familiar to many churches. With many local churches viewing other local churches as their competitors, due in part to the consumer mentality that church shoppers embody, many congregations feel enormous pressure to offer an ever-expanding variety of programs and services in order to attract and retain customers to their own version of the ecclesial supermarket. The result often looks less like the "one holy, catholic, and apostolic" church and more like the competing interest groups that fragment American social, political, and economic life.[21]

This symbiotic relationship between consumers of religion and marketers of religion is probably a classic example of the chicken and egg issue: It's difficult to know which came first. But now that both are firmly in place, it hardly matters. What does matter is that church marketing perpetuates this cycle by encouraging churches to meet felt needs and church shoppers to expect that those needs will be met. Hence, it comes as no surprise that one church marketer has written not only marketing guides for churches, but also a guide for church shoppers.[22]

The Dangers of "Consumer Confidence"

Ordinarily when economists speak of consumer confidence, they are referring to the ups and downs in consumer spending. Here, we are pointing to a different issue: the extraordinary confidence that church marketers place in the ability of consumers to determine for themselves what they need. At the heart of the marketing orientation, with its emphasis on felt needs, is an assumption that classical theological anthropology has flatly denied: that people can be trusted to know what is best for them. We have already noted that church marketers insist that the church try to meet the needs that people believe they have, not what the church believes they have (or ought to have). But central to the gospel is the news that God has graciously provided something that humanity didn't even know it needed. Because our lives have been warped by sin, we have alienated ourselves from God and placed ourselves in the position of being incapable of helping ourselves—and of even knowing what we truly need. But God did not wait until we expressed a need for God and then rush to meet that need. Rather, God reached out to us in the person of Jesus Christ while humanity remained trapped in its sin and rebellion against God (Romans 5). In an important sense, it was only as people were brought face-to-face with God in Jesus Christ that they came to understand their need to be in relationship with this God. This is certainly one of the implications of Jesus' numerous encounters with people as recorded in Scripture. For example, the Samaritan woman spoken of in John 4 does not come to Jesus looking for living water; rather, it is only as Jesus reaches out to her that she becomes aware that such a gift is available.

Church marketers are willing to grant such a point, and then go on to insist that Jesus also "met people where they were," a strategy they wish to imitate. This is a powerful argument, but we think it fails to do justice to the myriad ways Jesus responded to people. Yes, Jesus did meet some people "where they were," particularly when it appeared that meeting them there would likely provide an opportunity rather than an obstacle to taking them where Jesus wanted them to go. For example, it is striking that when the paralytic's friends bring him to Jesus, presumably to have him healed by Jesus, the latter does not heal him, but forgives his sins. It is only when the scribes accuse Jesus of blasphemy that Jesus offers as well to heal the paralytic. Yet Jesus clearly states that his reason for doing so is to convince the scribes that he has authority to forgive sins (Matt. 9:1-8).

Church marketers overlook that Jesus, in being faithful to his calling, also drove people away. Some of Jesus' most radical and disturbing teachings were given at those junctures when crowds were the largest (Luke 11:29ff; 14:25ff). Similarly, during his ministry Jesus recognized that he could not meet the needs that so many of his followers were clamoring for him to meet without at the same time denying who he was called by God to be. The temptations in the wilderness are just one example of his being tempted to deny his suffering-servant messiahship in the name of success and efficiency. It is noteworthy that none of the gospel accounts of Jesus' feeding the multitudes give any hint that this miracle was demanded by the crowds; Jesus decides that they should be fed. The Gospel of John notes that the crowds were so impressed with this miracle that they were planning to take Jesus by force to make him king, presumably because they well understood the implications of having such a resource at their disposal. But Jesus withdraws (John 6:15). When the crowds find him the next day, Jesus rebukes them for caring only about their bellies (6:26). They ask for a sign from Jesus, perhaps hoping for another free meal. But Jesus refuses, and launches instead into his famous "bread of life" discourse, in which he identifies himself with what they truly need. Many of his disciples find this teaching difficult, and many of them no longer follow Jesus after this point (6:60, 66).

The crowd's desire that Jesus feed them—that he meet their needs—and his subsequent refusal to do so suggest that his willing forays into meeting people's needs were inseparable from his desire that those activities point to who he was. In short, Jesus refused to carry out "the same" activity (feeding the crowds) for a different purpose (because the crowds wanted him to, both for selfish reasons and to legitimate their own understanding of messiahship), because he knew that doing so would be a denial of his calling. This suggests that Jesus understood that the activity of meeting needs could not be separated from questions of why those needs were being met and whether the way they were being met was commensurate with those ends. Once this larger framework that gives the church's meeting of needs its ultimate intelligibility is lost sight of, this activity of meeting needs is easily harnessed to other purposes and ends.

Left to ourselves, we do not know what we most need;

only God knows. It seems odd that twentieth-century Christians would need Nietzsche to remind us of this central tenet of the Christian faith:

> Christianity is a system, a *whole* view of things thought out together. By breaking one main concept out of it, the faith in God, one breaks the whole: nothing necessarily remains in one's hands. Christianity presupposes that man does not know, *cannot* know, what is good for him, what evil: he believes in God, who alone knows it.[23]

User-Friendly Churches

We have yet to see a serious discussion by church marketers about how the church is to discern which felt needs are legitimate. They seem to agree that all people's needs cannot be met at once, hence target marketing. One group of church marketers does acknowledge, though rather cursorily, that people may have needs that the church should not try to satisfy. However, the reasons for and examples of what they offer are less than fully illuminating. They write: "Persons may have wants that are not proper to satisfy, either because they go against society's interest (such as buying handguns) or against the consumers' long-term interests (such as cigarette smoking)."[24] It is disappointing that the marketers chose as examples two felt needs that churches are not usually expected to satisfy, since such examples fail to offer guidance about the crucial discernment churches must constantly make as they go about meeting people's needs. What do church marketers think about those felt needs that go against neither society's interest nor the consumers' long-term interests, but that may be at cross-purposes with God's interests, desires, and purposes? For example, what about the need many people have for the church to underwrite and legitimate their nationalistic fervor? Or what about the need many people have for the church to legitimate their middle-class, consumer lifestyles? Or what about the need many people have to be surrounded by people who are fundamentally like themselves with respect to race, class, marital and educational status, and the like? Should churches try to meet these felt needs? Church marketers offer little help in sorting through such difficult discernments. We think this lacuna is not simply an oversight. We think church marketers understand quite well that once one raises the likelihood that many felt needs of consumers are illegitimate and should not, therefore, be met by the church, then one has undermined one of the fundamental and sustaining principles of marketing: that we should strive to meet the needs that customers want met, not the ones that we or anyone else thinks they ought to want.

By not being up front about which felt needs should not be met and why, the church-marketing enterprise encourages the sending of mixed signals. In the best-case scenario, the church will in effect be saying to the Jan Mathenys of the world: "You need the church because the church can meet your needs, even though we will eventually have to tell you that some of those needs that you think are so important (and that you may have come here in order to have met) aren't needs that we plan on meeting. Indeed, part of what you need is to be told that some of your needs aren't genuine needs at all, but constructed needs of a sort that we intend to ignore." Since such a strategy of bait-and-switch will likely be met with incredulity if not anger and resentment, we doubt most churches will have the courage to actually follow through, even though those that do will likely send the Mathenys packing, looking for the church that will be less judgmental and more user-friendly.

CHAPTER FIVE

The Baby Boomerang

The Outreach Committee of First Church, having been assigned the task of coming up with an outreach plan for the coming year, met on the first Tuesday in September. Lyman Hensley, retired minister and chair of the committee, convened the meeting and began discussions regarding the church's options with regard to outreach and evangelism.

"It seems to me," he said, "that we are in a unique situation here at First Church. We have Christ College right across the street from us to the north, the Oakhurst subdivision to our west, and then Mill Town not one mile to the east. Given that configuration, we ought to decide which way we want to go."

John Hughes, Associate Professor of English at Christ College, removed his glasses, leaned back in his chair, and said, "Well, I think, given that we have so many students who worship with us, one of our first priorities ought to be to those students over there."

"Students can't help you build a church," said Bill

Lamant. "You know how transient they are, here today and gone tomorrow. No, what we need is more young couples with children. We've got a fine educational building here at the church."

"Not to mention the $3,800 a month payments that go with it," said Lyman.

"Right," said Bill, "and students aren't going to be able to contribute one dime toward that."

"But wait a minute," said John Hughes. "We've got to remember that although some students come and go, a lot of the leadership of this church today is made up of students who came here to church when they were students, graduated, and then got jobs in the community. We have to think of students in the long term."

"Well, that's a point," said Lyman. "But we do need more young couples, especially couples like those over in Oakhurst—young professionals with children."

"I'm not saying that we ought to ignore the students," said Bill. "Some of them are going to show up anyway. I'm just saying that if we want to have a growing church, we are going to have to reach people who have the resources to help us grow.

"And don't forget, we do have space limitations and only so much money for staff. If we focus on the students and do what needs to be done to get them here, we're going to lose space in the sanctuary for folks over in Oakhurst. Like it or not, those folks in Oakhurst aren't going to want to come here and crawl over students to find a seat. They've got cars, and they know how to find their way over to the Cloverdale Church."

Hazel Minor, who ran the federally supported day-care center in Mill Town, shifted in her seat. "What about Mill Town?" she asked. "Don't we have a tremendous opportunity to minister to those folks over there? People are always complaining about the drug and crime problems over there. Why don't we try to reach out to those folks?"

"You'd never get the Oakhurst folks in here if you were bringing in those Mill Town kids," said John. "I mean, like it or not, those are two very different kinds of people."

"We really need to do something over there," said Bill. "They do have a world of problems, but that community is different from us. For one thing, they prefer a much more emotional worship service, and they have a whole lot of situations we just can't relate to. We probably do need to do something, but I think they'd be better served if we did something over there."

"So we won't have to sit with them?" asked Hazel.

"Oh, come on, Hazel," said Lyman. "That's not the point, and you know it. It's just that if we're going to be successful in growing this church, we need to focus on people who are more like us than they are. After all, the people in Oakhurst need the church too. On top of that, they are closer to us than the Mill Town people."

"You mean you don't want to have to change to accommodate them?"

"It's not a matter of not wanting to change, Hazel," said Bill. "It's more a matter of time and resources. Most of us are busy in our own lives. We don't have time to deal with all of the problems that the Mill Town people have. We'd need a full-time person just to meet their needs."

"I just don't know how to relate to them," said Lyman. "You know better than any of us, Hazel, that they are so different from us. They have a whole different set of problems."

"And besides," said Bill, "if part of our concern is to raise the capital to pay for our new education wing, the Mill Town people aren't going to be any more helpful than the students."

"Maybe that shouldn't be our primary concern," said Hazel.

"Well, maybe it shouldn't," said Bill. "But we should have thought of that before we built the building. As it stands now, we've got a whopping debt retirement to consider, and neither the students nor the Mill Town folks are going to be much help in that."

"Well, if I'm hearing us correctly," said John Hughes, "One of our chief concerns is the debt on the new building. I've already said that I'm interested in the students. Why don't we make our primary objective that of reaching the Oakhurst folks and then bring in as many students as we can to help in our ministry to them?"

"What would we need to do to make the folks in Oakhurst aware of us?" asked Bill.

"And what about the students?" asked John Hughes.

Hazel leaned back in her chair and sighed.

We suspect that such a scenario is not uncommon in churches. Whether because of perceived limitations on resources, the makeup of a particular neighborhood or region, the desire to fulfill certain visions of what constitutes success in the church, cost-benefit analysis, or simply attitudes and fears, church leaders often restrict their evangelism and outreach ministries to particular groups of people. To be sure, such practices make the whole process of outreach and evangelism, particularly as many churches define those terms, much simpler. Church leaders come to believe that they can accomplish more with less if they will simply focus their efforts on one or two particular "types" of people.

Church marketing advocates sometimes capitalize on this putatively "natural" tendency of people to feel more comfortable associating with people who are "like" them. They encourage church leaders simply to continue in a more explicit and intentional manner to do what they are already doing. The trick is not to change anything but simply to approach the same task with more clearly defined goals and data.

To accomplish this goal, advocates of church marketing encourage church leaders to put into practice three related marketing processes: (1) segmenting, (2) targeting, and (3) positioning. In this chapter, we will briefly describe those processes and analyze the assumptions behind them.

Divide and Conquer

Segmenting, targeting, and positioning may be characterized as ways to divide and conquer particular portions of the population. Capitalizing on the differences among groups of people, church marketers promote the idea that churches are better off if they focus on certain parts of populations rather than on the population as a whole. They claim that populations can be broken down according to certain criteria and understood in ways that make the business of outreach and evangelism more manageable and efficient. This process, called segmenting, has been defined as "classifying the population into groups with different needs, characteristics or behaviors that will affect their reaction to a religious program or ministry offered to them."[1]

When the members of the evangelism and outreach committee of First Church divided the region around the church, they engaged in the act of segmenting. Even without the benefits of market research, they noticed that three separate groups of people lived in the vicinity of the church building and that these three groups of people were different in specifiable ways.

Furthermore, the members of the committee gave those differences paramount importance. What distinguished the Oakhurst suburbanites from the Christ College students and the Mill Towners were differences that really mattered, since they likely affected how each group might respond to the church's ministries and services. Moreover, these differences affected what the church could expect to gain or lose by reaching out to these groups of people.

Had the membership of the committee included an expert in marketing, he or she might have congratulated them for acknowledging that those differences mattered, in terms of both the church's ministry to them and the relative costs and benefits of such ministry for the church. The marketing expert also would have praised their wisdom in recognizing the relative disadvantages of trying to be "all things to all people."

The marketing expert likely would have encouraged them in the direction they were already going. They would have been told to target one segment or the best combination of segments and then develop ministries and marketing plans to meet the unique needs and interests of a particular segment. The committee could have chosen to aim at any of three segments and focus on that one particular segment. Or the committee could have chosen to focus on some combination of segments.

Having made the decision to focus on the Oakhurst subdivision as their primary target, the committee would then be encouraged to position the church relative to that target audience so that a favorable impression or image was created in the minds of the target audience that differentiated them from their church competitors and nonchurch competitors.

Should We Do What Comes Naturally?

In many ways, church marketing trades upon what appear to be the natural tendencies of people to group themselves along certain ethnic, political, and class lines. As such, church marketing simply extends what people do every day of their lives. But should the church encourage people to do "what comes naturally"?

We believe that appealing to what people "naturally" do as a basis for evangelism and mission is a mistake, for two reasons. First, labeling something as "natural" tends to obscure the interests that shape these activities. Second, these interests are often antithetical to the gospel.

When the Natural Really Isn't Natural

When the Outreach Committee members of First Church sat down to begin their planning for outreach and evangelism, they assumed that the population that surrounded the church was easily divided along certain lines. The Christ College students were different from the Oakhurst residents. The Mill Town people were different from them all. The committee regarded the important differences among these three groups strictly as a function of those particular people. In other words, the committee believed that the characteristics that differentiated the three groups were inherent to the groups themselves.

Of course, in some ways the committee was correct. The students did not have the economic resources that the Oakhurst residents had. The Mill Towners did witness more illegal drug use than either the students or the Oakhurst residents. However, what the committee did not recognize were the ways in which their own conscious and unconscious criteria worked to distinguish those groups. The committee failed to realize that they were not simply looking out at the world and seeing it as it really was. They came to their meeting knowing both how to distinguish people along certain lines and why those distinctions mattered. In other words, they failed to see the ways in which the distinctions they observed in the groups were really reflections of themselves.

The Outreach Committee members knew how to distinguish between the population segments before they began their meeting because our society, through its stories and practices, had taught them which similarities and distinctions among people matter. They knew who went with whom and who did not "mix." When they came to the meeting they already knew that the affluent Oakhursters would not want to be "put out" in any way. They knew that the students and the Mill Towners would not be able to help them economically. They agreed that there may be some long-term benefit in reaching the students, but not in reaching the Mill Towners. They knew all of this because our society teaches us how to make distinctions among groups of people.

The committee also knew why those distinctions between people mattered. As members of First Church, they wanted to accomplish certain goals and purposes. They had a new education building to pay for. They wanted to do as much as they could with the financial and staff resources allotted to them. They did not want to invest more time than necessary to reach the population. They wanted to grow in ways that ensured that the new people who came to the church would be similar to their congregation. They wanted to grow with as little disruption as possible. And they wanted to center their ministry in the buildings of First Church.

The goals of the committee, which were articulated in an informal way, influenced the value the committee placed on each segment of the population. Indeed, it seems as if the committee was engaging in a form of cost-benefit analysis. The Oakhursters appeared more valuable than the Mill Towners because the Oakhursters could be reached with the least amount of effort, change, and expense. In contrast, the Mill Towners could be reached only with a great deal of effort, change, and expense; in addition, the Mill Towners seemed to have little to offer in exchange. As a result, the Oakhurst group appeared to be the most obvious group to "evangelize."

When the Outreach Committee made their decision, they thought they did so on the basis of the "facts." The fact was that three different groups of people lived in the vicinity of First Church. The fact was that these differences among people were important and had to be honored. The fact was that the church's resources were limited, and they had a new building to pay for. Their attention to what the committee took to be the facts compelled them to decide in one way rather than another. Yet, as we will argue below, the "facts" were not simply the facts. In other words, what they took to be the facts of the matter were not self-evident in the ways they supposed.

When marketing advocates encourage the church to do "what comes naturally," they encourage the church to ignore the underlying criteria by which it ordinarily distinguishes between groups. They encourage us to note the differences that are already "there" and then to act on those differences by targeting certain groups. The committee at First Church had a wide range of options before them. However, the ways in which they perceived their neighborhood, the ways in which they thought about themselves as the church, and the ways in which they articulated their goals and values narrowed their range of options prematurely. While marketing practices do not create these "natural" ways of perceiving and acting in the world, they do reinforce them.

We believe that such "natural" practices conceal the ways

in which our society predisposes us to attend to some people and not to others. We tend to accept those culturally induced ways of seeing people as a function of "reality" and move on from there. Such concealment prevents us from uncovering the ways in which the world presses us into its own mold and keeps us from questioning the goals and motives that underlie our choices as to whom we will minister.

When the Natural Is Antithetical to the Gospel

A more disturbing problem with doing what comes naturally is that it encourages the creation and maintenance of homogeneous congregations. This is seen most clearly in the target marketing approach. Rather than offering an alternative to the social arrangements the world knows and reproduces, the church simply mimics those same arrangements. By relying on marketing activities (research, segmenting, targeting, positioning) to bring about change and growth, the congregation is excused from having to be genuinely transformed in order to reach the world. The unspoken message of target marketing is that the church need not be different from the world; it simply needs to package itself differently, position itself properly, and enjoy the benefits that come from engaging in mutually beneficial exchanges with its target market.

Many church marketers admit that their approach tends to encourage homogeneous communities, but deny that this is a problem. Indeed, some suggest that targeted and homogeneous communities are God's plan for reaching a heterogeneous population.

It is not biblically improper or indefensible to have many churches in the same community. It is entirely possible that the reason God allows His people to be separated among so many different congregations is because He realizes each group, strategically speaking, will reach a relatively small proportion of the total population. Each congregation, then, represents another resource available for penetrating a given sector of the population.

If every church truly operated from a base of God's vision, we would likely see a community in which a mosaic of purposes and target audiences resided among those churches. As each church responded obediently to God's vision for ministry, they would reach their market. One church might effectively penetrate the white baby buster market with a traditional style; another might reach the same people group, but with a contemporary style; still a third church might appeal to nonwhite busters. One church might be best equipped to attract single baby boomers, another better poised to reach boomers who are married and have young children.

Should these churches consciously exclude people who are outside their target group? Absolutely not. However, because different population segments respond to different ministry opportunities, marketing stimuli and the like, focusing marketing efforts on a target group allows for a more efficient attraction of that market.[2]

In a world immersed in the marketing mentality, such an argument appears defensible, even reasonable. But is such an approach actually rooted in God's vision for the church? We don't believe so. Notice, for example, the willingness to divide the church along culturally prescribed lines: white baby busters who prefer a traditional style, white baby busters who prefer a contemporary style, and nonwhite busters. Notice also the willingness to exclude (unconsciously) people outside the target group in the name of more "efficient attraction." According to the marketing mentality, part of what makes consumers different is that they have different tastes, preferences, and styles. If you want to attract a certain segment of consumers, you should focus on appealing to their tastes and preferences, realizing that in doing so you will likely alienate other segments. Trying to create a product that appeals to everyone is futile. Indeed, many advocates of church marketing appeal to the apostle Paul's words in 1 Corinthians 9:19-23—that he became like a Jew to the Jews and like a Gentile to the Gentiles—as a sanction for their targeting approach.[3]

Yet this way of describing the challenges facing the church from cultural pluralism wrongly identifies them as simply issues of style and preference, rather than as issues central to the gospel. Granted, people do respond more favorably to those who understand them and "speak their language." Here, Paul's example is instructive. But Paul would have been mortified had someone suggested that people would be attracted more efficiently if Jews and Gentiles were encouraged to develop separate congregations to cater to their own styles. Paul would have regarded such a strategy as fundamentally at cross-purposes with the message of the gospel and the radically new way of thinking and acting demanded by those who had been grasped by it.

In many of his letters, Paul speaks of the gospel as having a definite and visible social shape. In the first century, this was embodied in the unprecedented practice of table fellowship among Jews and Gentiles. In Christ, Jews and Gentiles had been incorporated into one new humanity where these previously all-important and defining differences no longer mattered (Gal. 3:28; 5:6; 6:15; Eph. 2:11-22; Col. 3:11). As René Padilla writes:

> Those who have been baptized "into one body" (1 Cor 12:13) are members of a community in which the differences that separate people in the world have become obsolete. It may be true that "men like to become Christians without crossing racial, linguistic or class barriers," but that is irrelevant. Membership in the body of Christ is not a question of likes or dislikes, but a question of incorporation

into a new humanity under the lordship of Christ. Whether a person likes it or not, the same act that reconciles one to God simultaneously introduces the person into a community where people find their identity in Jesus Christ rather than in their race, culture, social class, sex, and are consequently reconciled to one another. . . . God's purpose is to bring the universe "into a unity in Christ" (Eph 1:10 NEB). That purpose is yet to be consummated. But already, in anticipation of the end, a new humanity has been created in Jesus Christ, and those who are incorporated in him form a unity wherein all the divisions that separate people in the old humanity are done away with. The original unity of the human race is thus restored; God's purpose of unity in Jesus Christ is thus made historically visible.[4]

There are powerful reasons to think that congregations that are culturally segregated are an affront to, if not an embodied denial of, the gospel. And this is true whether that segregation is premised upon differences in race, gender, social class, marital status, or generation. Once again, we want to acknowledge that church marketing did not create the segregated church in the United States; the church has always had difficulty embodying a gospel that breaks down the dividing walls of hostility separating people. But to sanction the rebuilding of these walls in the name of attracting people is to forget who we have been called to be. If the church is to be a sign, a foretaste, and a herald of a new humanity that God is bringing into being, a humanity in which the cultural barriers that matter in the world are torn down, then the church cannot, in the name of mission and outreach, encourage people to simply do what comes naturally.

Further Along the Marketing Way

Of course, advocates of church marketing could argue that congregations are not compelled to segment populations along such "natural" lines. First Church could have chosen the Mill Towners or the students as their primary targets. They could have decided to serve all single mothers, whether they were from Oakhurst, from the college, or from Mill Town. In this case, however, that would have required significant adjustment of goals. Yet they were not required to divide the population in ways that appeared natural.

Dividing the population along less natural lines would still require criteria for slicing the pie one way instead of another. Such criteria have been developed by church-marketing advocates. They suggest, among other things, that (1) market segments be measurable, (2) that they be accessible to the church's ministries, (3) that they be substantial in size, and (4) that they be responsive to the church's offerings.[5] On the surface, these criteria may sound harmless enough. However, if we examine the assumptions that underwrite those criteria, we see how they might distort the mission of the church.

Measurement

The practice of marketing involves the continual gathering and assessment of information about potential target markets. As Barna writes:

> Because niche strategies depend upon access to a substantial amount of reliable and detailed information, do not select a segment about which little is, or will be, known. You need consistent updates of data on the size of a market segment, how they live and think, and what their needs are.[6]

Church-marketing advocates constantly encourage churches to be as data driven as possible. A marketing expert would tell First Church to consult with community leaders about the makeup of the Oakhurst community and to survey and interview as many of the actual residents as possible to get a better handle on the residents' needs, interests, and lifestyles. The more reliable the data, the greater the likelihood that the church will be able to repackage itself in ways that will appeal to the residents of Oakhurst.

Such a perspective presupposes that data, like the daisies in the Oakhurst residents' yards, are simply out there for the picking. What such a view conceals is the whole question as to what constitutes data. In other words, how are the members of First Church to know data when they see it?

Data are not simply "given." Data only become data as they serve particular ends or purposes. And because data only become data as they serve particular ends, data are really clusters of concealed "values."[7] For example, the members of the Outreach Committee decided to evangelize the Oakhurst community, because the Oakhurst people could best help First Church to meet its goals. Therefore, the Oakhurst residents have a certain value to First Church that neither the students nor the Mill Towners have.

Having decided to go after the Oakhursters, the Outreach Committee must now decide which attributes of that community they need to measure. Chances are very good that they will not decide to count the number of blondes in Oakhurst, because knowing that will not help them achieve the goals that inform their search. However, they may well want to determine which of the Oakhursters are church shopping as opposed to settled already in churches. Further, they will want to know which of the Oakhursters are already favorably inclined to the church as opposed to those who have absolutely no interest in the church at all. That there are a certain number of blondes in Oakhurst may be data of a sort, but it is not data to the members of First Church, unless one of the church's goals is to minister to persons of a particular hair color.

What this means, in effect, is that while the committee canvasses the Oakhurst community for data to help them understand Oakhurst, they do so not with a magnifying glass but with a mirror. What they find and what they call data is little more than traces of the things people of First Church hold dear. They do not and could not simply look for data on Oakhurst. Instead, they are looking for traces of themselves and of their own convictions and values.

To be sure, the traces they find in Oakhurst, the so-called data, will have a tremendous influence on the Outreach Committee. After they compile their findings, they will create impressive graphs and charts and tables of numbers. And those artifacts will exercise a tremendous influence on their decisions as they go about serving the Oakhurst community—not simply because they have ascertained the residents' needs, but because the committee has arrived at those conclusions "scientifically." Decisions will not be made, or so they believe, on the basis of feelings, opinions, or interests. The charts and graphs will reassure them that they are making their decisions objectively.

That the members of the Outreach Committee believe such things suggests how captivated they are by certain widespread habits of thought. Every school-aged child is drilled to know that data and facts are more important, more weighty than opinions and values. Yet, what few school children are told is that all data and all facts present themselves as such only against the backdrop of shared agreements about particular ends and purposes. For example, marketing advocates often comment that there are roughly 76 million "baby boomers" in the United States. This fact, however, is premised on the debatable assumption that persons born between 1946 and 1964 share enough of a common cultural heritage to be identified as a generation. In a similar way, boomers are often claimed to be "the most educated generation in history," though such an assertion requires that we agree about what counts as "educated." The ways in which convictions shape data collection can also be demonstrated by observing that despite the U.S. government's fixation on statistical studies, no statistics are kept about social class or caste in the United States, presumably because we pride ourselves in thinking that such divisions do not exist or at least do not matter.

Such observations should serve as a warning to churches that decide to gather data on their community as a tool for ministry. Certainly things might be learned that could inform a congregation's planning. Yet churches must also recognize that data gathering isn't as innocent as it looks. The entire enterprise is laden with convictions that may or may not be at cross-purposes with its own self-understanding and mission. Those churches that clearly recognize these dangers may be less willing to hitch their entire ministry to a set of numbers.

Accessibility

Advocates of church marketing also suggest that churches select their segments in terms of how accessible those segments are to the church's ministry. In discussing which segments the church should choose, Barna offers this advice:

> Be sure they are reachable. Some segments are attractive but finding them is next to impossible. One church wanted to minister to women who had experienced abortions or the loss of a child. How do you find these women? Another congregation was hoping to locate and attract community residents who were substance abusers. Once again, not a readily available market.[8]

On the surface, this suggestion makes good sense. After all, why try to reach those who are difficult to find when there are plenty of people in need of the church right under your nose, especially if they can be reached without depleting scarce resources?

100

We know church marketers have a passion, as we do, for reaching all people with the gospel. However, we believe that judgments concerning accessibility are often grounded in faulty assumptions. One of those assumptions has to do with the nature of accessibility. Church marketing advocates often seem to suggest that accessibility is a characteristic of the targeted population. They write as if certain segments of the population are somehow inherently more difficult to locate and to serve than are others.

In contrast, we believe that accessibility is not a characteristic of particular targeted populations so much as it is of those who target them. We believe, to use Barna's examples, that women who have had abortions or who have lost children or residents who are substance abusers are accessible if the congregation is willing to expend the necessary time, effort, and money to reach them. But that is precisely the rub. Church marketers consistently depict the church as those people who must operate efficiently with scarce resources of time, money, and personnel. They consistently encourage the church to use those limited resources in ways that deliver "more bang for the buck." Such a strategy is often defended in the name of good stewardship, though one has to wonder whether this is the only motivating factor when those persons who can be reached most cost effectively are often also those who happen to be remarkably like us.

Hazel Minor, the one lone advocate for the residents of Mill Town, made a very good point when she suggested that the reason why First Church did not want to reach the Mill Towners was because they would have to change in order to do so. Bringing people like the Mill Towners into First Church would require expenditures of resources as well as changes in attitudes and behaviors. The members of First Church would have to overcome certain prejudices and fears. But those "costs" were deemed too high, which is the

SELLING OUT THE CHURCH

primary reason why the Oakhurst residents seemed more reachable to the Outreach Committee of First Church. Oakhurst residents could be assimilated into First Church at little cost. Here we see how judgments of accessibility often say more about those making the judgments than they do about those upon whom the judgments are made.

Substantiality

Some church marketing advocates suggest that segments be selected that are of substantial size to justify the church's efforts. Barna claims:

> The market you select as your target should be large enough to enable you to survive. If you select a segment that is too tiny you will spend an enormous amount of resources attempting to reach and minister to a group that cannot provide the necessary economies of scale to justify being targeted.[9]

And another group of marketers writes:

> Substantiality . . . is the degree to which the resulting segments are large enough to be worth pursuing. The pastoral counseling center may decide that white affluent female drug addicts are too few in number to be worth the development of a special treatment and marketing program.[10]

In advocating substantiality as one of the criteria by which to select segments, church marketers seem to advise simple prudence. However, we question the bases upon which such prudence is advanced.

As we noted in chapter 3, marketing takes "exchange" as a first principle. The church is described as offering goods and services in exchange for attendance and offerings of money, time, and effort. The aim of such exchange is to improve the lot of both the church and the targeted segment. That practice implies that one of the principle aims of marketing generally and of targeting segments of substantial size particularly is to ensure that the church survive and thrive. That the well-being of the church is of paramount concern to marketing advocates is easily demonstrated. One group of marketers writes: "The purpose of marketing is to help organizations ensure survival and continued health through serving their markets more effectively."[11] Barna, in the quotation above, suggests that the church must consider its own survival and the "necessary economies of scale" in selecting a marketing segment and, therefore, place the self-interest of the church before the ministry the church could offer to certain groups. The other marketers quoted cast potential ministry in terms of worth and make the potential service to female drug addicts a matter of whether such service can pay off for the pastoral counseling center. When criteria such as substantiality enter into decisions concerning to whom the church will minister, the congregation places its own well-being before its ministry.

What is particularly bothersome about this are the ways in which the church's well-being is so easily equated with institutional well-being. Granted, most churches are not likely or willing to ask whether their high overhead inhibits their ability to reach people for the kingdom. Yet such questions certainly beg to be asked, particularly in this country, where countless billions of dollars are tied up in church properties and investments in ways that often inhibit ministry as much as they enhance it. Again, we do not suggest that congregations never engaged in cost-benefit analysis before church marketing arrived on the scene. Yet churches may still want to pause and consider whether they desire to travel even further down this road, as marketing seems to encourage. Churches that have incurred high overhead costs will have to decide how to pay for them. But one still might wonder whether we should encourage Christians to weigh the benefits the institutional church is likely to reap before they decide whether they can afford to reach out to a particular group of people. Such cost-benefit analysis seems odd for a body of people who follow the one who suggested that leaving the ninety-nine sheep to search for the one lost sheep is perfectly reasonable within the logic of God's kingdom.

Responsiveness

Some church marketing advocates claim that the church should target segments on the basis of how responsive they are likely to be. These church marketers argue that there is little reason to exert too much effort if the segment has a history of being unresponsive to the church's overtures. In this regard, Barna asks:

> Is there a reasonable prospect for success? If your church will live or die on the balance of bringing homeless people into the congregation, you may want to reevaluate that segment as being your dominant market. Some segments simply do not hold enough promise of success to justify putting all of your eggs into that basket. Toward that end you ought to have a sense of what has been done by other organizations seeking to capture the loyalty of a given segment before you identify them as your target group.[12]

We remain uncomfortable with the notion that the church should be in the business of determining who is and who isn't likely to respond to the gospel. We get even more nervous when this idea is coupled with segmenting, for then the church is placed in the position of discerning whether whole segments are likely to be responsive or unresponsive. But church marketers seem to have no such qualms. In fact, Barna sees Jesus' parable of the sower in Matthew 13 as supporting the practice of segmenting according to the criterion of responsiveness:

The parable of the sown seeds (Matthew 13) portrays marketing the faith as a process in which there are hot prospects and not-so-hot prospects and shows how we should gear our efforts toward the greatest productivity. This is the essence of target marketing—recognizing the various segments of the audience, and treating marketing as an ongoing process. Some people are ready for conversion, others are not.[13]

This appears to us to be a very strange reading of the Gospel text. Barna is at best only half right: This parable does remind us that some people accept the gospel, and some don't. But what Barna believes follows from this is exactly the opposite of what the gospel seems to suggest. Barna believes that such a recognition demands that we calculate who is ready for the gospel and who isn't, sowing seed only where we suspect it will grow. But the sower in the Gospel text doesn't do this at all. Instead, the sower sows seed recklessly. Barna is right: Some people are ready for conversion, and others are not. But the mistake is in thinking that we are in a position to know which people fall into which camp. Perhaps even more disturbing is the suggestion by marketers that these two groups—those who are ready and those who are not—somehow conform to the ways in which they have segmented the population. Isn't it a little odd to suggest, for example, that the Oakhursters (as a group) are somehow ready for the gospel, while the Mill Towners (as a group) are resistant?

In characterizing the Mill Town people as different and difficult, the Outreach Committee of First Church, with perhaps the exception of Hazel Minor, placed the resistance or the lack of responsiveness upon the residents of Mill Town. In so doing, the committee deflected the concerns that Hazel raised and also avoided the hard questions they should have asked themselves. Rather than ask whether they had spent and were spending their resources of time, money, and energy wisely, they simply magnified the differences between them and the Mill Town residents so that their decision not to reach out to them became a foregone conclusion.

The Baby Boomerang?

When churches like First Church sit down to determine the direction they ought to go in evangelism and outreach, they engage in acts of discernment. They evaluate options and make judgments as to how the church ought to go about that task and with whom. Of course, it is inevitable that churches engage in this process, for even those churches that appear to do nothing with regard to outreach do make judgments, if only by default, about their direction in that regard.

Discernment is never carried out in a vacuum. Instead, churches and church leaders discern direction for the church in some context, on the basis of some criterion, and in the light of some goal. Sometimes church leaders are conscious of those contexts, criteria, and goals. Sometimes they are not. Sometimes the goals and criteria are selected by default, as in the case of reaching out to groups on the basis of their so-called natural differences. Sometimes the goals and criteria are more intentionally selected, as when a church formally adopts the marketing approach. However, those factors always enter into the process of discernment. That is why we believe that it is critical to examine the assumptions behind the practices of segmenting, targeting, and positioning. Like boomerangs, the consequences of such methods may come back around to the church, although now in ways that distort the church's message and character.

CHAPTER SIX

Create Your Own Future!

PART OF WHAT MAKES THE FUTURE THE future is that it is different from the present. Part of what makes the future threatening is that the difference the future brings is never entirely predictable. The future, by virtue of being the future, always involves the surprising, the novel, the unforeseen. As a species of management, marketing attempts to control or to manage this unpredictable future by domesticating its inherent risks. Since the church is not immune to these risks, it is understandable that its leaders might be tempted to employ marketing, along with other management practices, as a measure of control over a seemingly chaotic future.

But the pressure on the pastor to be a manager or marketer stems not simply from concern about the future. Equally important, this role has evolved in the midst of a society in which the pastor's position as local theologian has declined, if not evaporated. Gone are the days when people respected pastors primarily for their theological insight and learning. As British sociologist Bryan Wilson suggests, this shift in roles is directly related to the diminished regard for theology:

What the priest is expert in—the knowledge of God—is simply no longer regarded, in practice, as very important in

107

our society. It is not practical knowledge; it will not stand up to the pragmatic tests of the age; it accomplishes nothing. It does not even necessarily make a good clergyman in an age which demands that he be a general affective agent rather than a constructor of sermons. He has lost his identification with the educational system in the last sixty years as sacred and secular knowledge have grown apart and as theology has lost its claim to be basic to all other knowledge.[1]

Thus within a secularized culture of experts, the professional pastor must seek out a realm of expertise that is considered relevant by his or her consumers. This, coupled with Wilson's observation that the pastor is expected to function primarily as "a general *affective* agent," helps to account for the increasing number of prominent pastor-therapists and pastor-managers.[2] Both models presuppose that the pastor's job is to manage the affective, or emotional, lives of his or her constituents. The pastor-therapist does this primarily on the individual level, while the pastor-manager does this largely on the corporate level. Both are involved in managing how their constituencies feel about themselves and their lives, including their participation in congregational life.[3]

The advocates of church marketing insist (rightly, we suppose) that pastors have not been adequately equipped by their seminaries to function in their newly acquired roles as marketers/managers. As Barna writes:

The average pastor has been trained in religious matters. Yet, upon assuming church leadership, he is asked to run a business! Granted, that business is a not-for-profit organization, but it is still a business. The church is in the business of ministry: searching out people who need the gift of acceptance, forgiveness, and eternal life that is available in knowing Jesus Christ. For the local church to be a successful business, it must impact a growing share of its market area.

Ultimately, many people do judge the pastor not on his ability to preach, teach, or counsel, but on his capacity to make the church run smoothly and efficiently. In essence, he is judged as a businessman, an area in which he has received no training or preparation. In fact, even the pastor's ability to use his training in religious matters hinges on his business capabilities. He must be a good enough businessman to keep the church solvent and make it appealing enough for people to attend before he has the chance to impact their lives.[4]

Here we see marketing and managing being offered not simply as activities that might enhance a church's ministry, but as the hub around which everything else turns. Indeed, Barna seems to suggest that if a pastor isn't first of all a savvy manager or marketer, everything else he or she does will be in vain. What is it about management in general, and marketing as a species of management, that would compel us to place them at the center of ministry?

Control, Measurement, and Effectiveness

Management purports to bring a measure of control and order to potentially chaotic situations. Indeed, a cursory glance at the titles of books and articles about management suggest that this "science" is dedicated to bringing a measure of control and order to those areas of our lives where either we feel most out of control (risk management, conflict management, crisis management, stress management) or we sense the importance of exercising control over "scarce resources" (time management, personnel management, money management). In keeping with this spirit, one group of church marketers writes: "Marketing is defined as a managerial process involving analysis, planning, implementation, and control."[5]

This definition is instructive. It suggests that the control and order that marketing promises are closely tied to the process of marketing itself. In other words, marketing purports to bring order by being orderly itself.

> One of the beauties of marketing is that it is an orderly process. It is not a series of random, spontaneous actions that magically result in profitable enterprise. Whenever marketing has played a significant role in an episode of business success, that success can be traced to the fact that all of the marketing activities were systematically undertaken in accordance with a preconceived idea of how to approach the opportunities inherent in the environment. Marketing, then, is a systematic series of active responses to existing conditions that is geared toward reaching specific goals.[6]

But the marketer knows it is not enough to promise a greater measure of control and order; that control and order must themselves yield certain desired results. Perhaps more accurately, we consider people to have brought order or control only if they can demonstrate that they have brought about certain desired results. This suggests that the marketer's authority rests almost solely on his or her ability to deliver promised results, what we often call "effectiveness." Such effectiveness is usually thought to be a manifestation of the ability of managers and marketers to collect and analyze information in ways that make human behavior predictable. MacIntyre writes:

> The claim that the manager makes to effectiveness rests of course on the further claim to possess a stock of knowledge by means of which organizations and social structures can be molded. Such knowledge would have to include a set of factual law-like generalizations which would enable the manager to predict that, if an event or state of affairs of a certain type were to occur or to be brought about, some other event or state of affairs of some specific kind would result. For only such law-like generalizations could yield those particu-

lar causal explanations and predictions by means of which the manager could mold, influence and control the social environment.[7]

Church marketers routinely imply that such predictability is one of the benefits of marketing. For example, when Barna is touting the importance of gathering information about people's attitudes, he remarks that "knowing their thinking can help you predict their behavior, or establish a means of ministering to them more effectively given their mind-set."[8] But even though predictability is important to marketers, it is not desired for its own sake; rather, the conclusion of Barna's sentence points to the central promise, repeated in all of the marketing literature: Marketing will make any organization *more effective*. Hence, one group of church marketers, after listing six "essential marketing concepts," goes on to assert that "these concepts, when applied, are almost certain to make a ministry more effective."[9] Similarly, Stevens and Loudon write:

> The basic reason an organization should be interested in applying marketing principles is that they will enable it to achieve its objectives more effectively. Organizations in our country depend upon voluntary exchanges to accomplish their objectives. Marketing is the discipline concerned with managing exchanges effectively and efficiently.[10]

Predictability, therefore, is at the service of effectiveness. But how does one know or demonstrate that one is being more effective by employing marketing? Here we are reminded that marketing is a systematic process of management that has built into it an evaluation step. As one group of marketers writes, "Evaluation is an essential ingredient of marketing control" whose purpose "is to increase program effectiveness and aid in future planning."[11] But it would be a mistake to think that evaluation is merely the final step in

111

the marketing process; in fact, it would not be overstating the matter to say that evaluation shapes every step of the process. The impact of evaluation is seen clearly in the setting of objectives, as Stevens and Loudon point out:

> The objectives in the marketing plan become the yardsticks used to evaluate performance. . . . It is impossible to evaluate performance without some standard with which results can be compared. The objectives become the standards for evaluating performance because they are the statement of results desired by the planner.[12]

Thus, because the church knows at the outset that at some future date it will need to evaluate the effectiveness of its ministry programs, it needs to set objectives for those programs that will lend themselves to being evaluated in measurable terms. In short, marketers and managers believe that you can evaluate only what you can measure (or in the terms of the social sciences, what you can "operationalize"). This is why marketers insist that sound management practice requires that an organization specify measurable objectives that will serve as a means to achieve that organization's goals. Stevens and Loudon claim: "Marketing objectives can be defined as clear, concise written statements outlining what is to be accomplished in key areas in a certain time period, in objectively measurable terms that are consistent with overall organizational objectives."[13] Barna also insists that a church's vision, "when translated into marketing objectives, should be defined in specific and measurable statements."[14]

We noted in the previous chapter the important role that measurement plays in the process of segmentation. But the centrality of measurement is not limited to that one process. To see how important the notion of measurement is to the marketing orientation, we have listed below several marketing objectives that have been written by church marketers as ways of operationalizing certain goals churches may have. According to church marketers, such objectives are the heart and soul of a church's marketing plan:

GOAL:
Expose young people to the gospel
OBJECTIVES:
- See 50 baby busters accept Christ as their Savior within 1 year, at a total cost of $5,000.
- Generate a 10 percent increase in the number of young adults in the church who read the Bible daily; budget—$1,000.

GOAL:
Provide opportunities to put Christian love into action
OBJECTIVES:
- Help 5 homeless people get jobs and housing within 1 year; allocate $7,500 for this outreach.
- Sponsor 3 needy overseas children by the end of the year, at a maximum of $25 a month.

GOAL:
Teach God's Word without compromise to an increasing number of people
OBJECTIVES:
- Expand total Sunday School attendance to 300 adults, 250 kids on an average weekend; the aggregate cost of this expansion, for marketing, materials, and other resources, should be $3,000 or less.
- Increase participation in small groups to 20 adult groups with 200 adults; 10 teen groups with 100 teens; the expansion should cost the church $750 or less.[15]

Marketers understand that the appeal of their approach is closely tied to the widespread fixation people have with control, measurement, and effectiveness. On the surface, these emphases and the ways marketers discuss and implement them appear rather innocuous at worst and positively beneficial at best. The rest of this chapter seeks to expose the assumptions underwriting these concepts and the ways in which they threaten the church's self-understanding.

Problematic Assumptions

As noted earlier, church marketers operate with a strong distinction between form and content, between means and ends, and between method and theology. They are convinced that the marketing forms, means, and methods that they are promoting carry with them no theological freight. This is underscored by the way in which church marketers casually refer to their form of ministry as just one more "style":

> What perturbs me is when people with a particular style of ministry get upset because they hear somebody promoting a different style. Many of my critics miss the difference between theology and methodology. Scripture is abundantly clear theologically, but it gives enormous latitude methodologically. If your theology and your heart are right, you have many different ways to promote the gospel and penetrate culture.[16]

We haven't missed the distinction marketers make between theology and methodology. Indeed, this strong distinction is part of what we find so problematic. In saying this, we are not suggesting that there is only *one* appropriate way to "promote the gospel and penetrate culture." Rather, we are arguing that certain ways of managing the future, such as "management by objective," or "total quality management," are not theologically neutral. But church marketers clearly think their methods are harmless, partly because they continue to think that a church's polity—the way a church is organized and structured—is theologically insignificant. Here Robert Jenson's comments about the separation of theology and polity in the Lutheran tradition are instructive:

> [It was assumed] that questions of polity are neutral with respect to the gospel, and may safely be left to those who enjoy organizing things. . . . We have generally supposed that questions of polity were not to be argued by theological considerations, but by considerations of "efficiency." The result has regularly been that Lutheran polity has merely imitated—usually about fifteen years behind—the sort of organization currently dominant in society. . . . We have thereby merely accepted that bondage to the world's example from which the gospel is supposed to free us.[17]

We believe that church marketers, though well meaning, are unwittingly introducing the church to a new form of cultural bondage. Church marketers believe that the church is a business and that the business model supplies the necessary images and metaphors for directing the church's thinking and acting. If other businesses have benefited from applying management principles (including marketing), then there is no reason to think the church wouldn't also benefit. Yet some of the concepts and assumptions of management and marketing theory are ill fitted for the church's unique mission in the world. Church marketing, by embodying certain cultural convictions, shackles the Body of Christ by insisting that the church attempt to control and manage the future. The interlocking convictions that comprise these chains, and the ways in which they bind the church, warrant careful consideration.

Should the Church Try to Manage the Future?

The church is called to live with an eye on the future, but not in the way that marketing does. Marketers attempt to manage the future in order to reduce the risk involved in making decisions in the face of that uncertain future. Bad decisions translate into lost market shares, which translate into lost profits for stakeholders. The church also understands that the future always brings risk, but these risks are of a different character. For example, the church understands that it is always one generation away from extinction and that it must reproduce through witness the church of tomorrow. But it is not enough that the church merely exist tomorrow; the church must itself be of a certain character in order to serve its purpose in the world as God's embodied witness. Hence, the future always brings the temptation of unfaithfulness. But these risks cannot be managed or reduced; they are part of the fabric of the church's existence. Indeed, the church may be in no greater danger than when it is led to believe that these risks are under control.

Marketers and managers might agree with this assessment, yet still insist that the church would be better off if its day-to-day affairs and decision making were structured according to management and marketing principles. After all, as Barna's quotation reminded us earlier in this chapter, many people are judging the pastor on his or her "capacity to make the church run smoothly and efficiently." We suspect Barna is correct in this assessment; people do judge the church on this basis. But, we are tempted to ask, should they? Even more to the point, should the church encourage them to do so by trying to make the church run smoothly and efficiently, like a well-oiled machine? Is that part of the character of the church's identity?

As we noted earlier, management is typically appealed to in one of two situations: first, when events are threatening to get out of control (crisis management), and second, when resources are scarce (resource management). But again, we are not sure that the church is better off when it faces these situations with management and marketing principles in hand. We know of many pastors who have been trained in forms of "conflict management" and who thereby assume that conflicts in the church can and should be managed (which usually means suppressed or even defused before they arise). But the church does not (or at least should not) fear conflict the way the world does. For example, a church that grasps the pervasiveness of sin, God's bountiful grace, and its own character as both forgiving and forgiven will approach conflict in a quite different spirit. As the account of the Jerusalem Council in Acts 15 demonstrates, conflict can be the occasion for edification rather than destruction. But this is true only when the church understands its peculiar character.[18]

If managers want their organizations to run smoothly, marketers want theirs to run efficiently. As noted earlier, many promote target marketing in the name of efficiency. Moreover, church marketers insist that one of the benefits of marketing is that it provides a superior method of managing scarce resources:

> Every church is plagued by limited resources: human, financial, and physical. But these limitations do not have to limit what you accomplish. If you know exactly where you're going and how you're going to get there, it is much easier not only to conserve your readily available resources and use them more efficiently, but also to identify other needed resources and determine how to acquire them.[19]

No doubt the marketers would say this is simply realism. But we are not sure that the church is called to be "realistic" in this way. Why should the church, which exists to serve and witness to the God of the universe, whose Spirit dwells within it, begin with the assumption that it is "plagued by limited resources"? Why should we begin by focusing on what we seemingly lack rather than on the graciousness and sufficiency of the God we serve? (See Philippians 4:19).

We suspect that church marketers would reply that their drive for efficiency is nothing more than a concern for stewardship. Some, for example, are very up-front that marketing is a "stewardship issue," since "if a church isn't consciously engaged in marketing, it's probably not being a good steward of its resources."[20] Yet stewardship is a slippery concept in this context. The logic seems to be that because our resources are scarce, and because we are stewards of these resources, we must make the most efficient use of them, which, according to the marketers, requires the use of marketing. Yet the gospel of Jesus Christ is rooted in an economy of plenty, not an economy of scarcity. God lavishes good gifts on the creation in ways that defy the stinginess inherent in the economy of scarcity and efficiency. Efficiency demands producing desired results with the least expenditure of time, energy, money, and other resources. Yet is this kind of efficiency a fundamental operating principle of the kingdom of God? Is this what the church has been called to bear witness to? Robert Lupton offers a powerful reminder to the contrary:

> The Church is the only institution which, without irresponsibility, can expend all its resources on great and lavish outbursts of compassion. It is ordained to give itself away, yet without loss. The Church, above all earthly symbols, bears the responsibility of declaring in the outpouring of resources, the utter dependability of God. To preserve its life is to lose it.[21]

When efficiency is the primary virtue, achieving the desired results is what matters. And as the marketers insist, this requires knowing where you want to go and how you're going to get there. But the church has good reasons to believe that it need not know where God is leading or how to get there. What God *has* entrusted to us is partial responsibility for who we become along the way, regardless of the destination or the itinerary. From this perspective, it becomes more difficult to determine what efficiency means. If God believed it was necessary for the children of Israel to wander forty years in the wilderness in order to learn to trust in God rather than in themselves, who are we to come along and say that this is a very inefficient way to get to the promised land? Such a judgment would have to assume that getting to the promised land was the only thing that mattered, though it seems clear from Scripture that who the people would be when they got there was enormously important to God.

This leads us to another danger of appropriating management theory in the church: The whole notion of management encourages us to think that *we* are in control. By so doing, marketing encourages the church to place its trust in its own marketing savvy rather than in God. Marketers insist that the church needs to determine where it's going and how it's going to get there. But what if the church, like Abraham, has been called to embark on a pilgrimage to an unknown destination, a pilgrimage that requires dependence upon and trust in God rather than ourselves? What if marketers insist that we begin with a vision of the future that the church believes that it not only cannot have but also should not desire or seek? How do we leave ourselves open to the guidance of the Spirit if every step in the marketing process is based strictly on human wisdom?

Marketers say that their approach does not preempt God's guidance. In fact, several of them insist that they want to leave room for the Spirit. Yet we wonder how they envision this taking place. It's not that we think God couldn't work through this approach. But we do wonder where, in the process of marketing, God is allowed to guide or to act. One group of marketers insists that they are not implying "that good marketing is all that is needed to generate religious exchanges. We are aware of the Divine admonition that success comes 'not by might, nor by power, but by my spirit, says the Lord of hosts' (Zech. 4:6)." They then go on to explain that Zechariah's words remind them of certain types of biblical examples, such as the Lord's telling Moses to send spies into the land of Canaan. They write: "While God might have revealed this information to the Israelites in a dream, He chose to have them use their own powers of observation, analysis, and planning to obtain and use this data."[22]

What is fascinating to us about their use of this example is that they don't tell the whole story. They give the impression that God encouraged the children of Israel to do a little marketing research so that their decision-making process would be informed by accurate and objective information about their environment. But they do not mention that there were twelve spies and that ten of them convinced the majority of the Israelites that, based on their conclusive "research," they had no hope of occupying the land that the Lord *had already promised to give them*. Even though Caleb (and later Joshua) spoke in favor of trusting the Lord to fulfill that promise, the people accepted the majority research report and subsequently complained to God for bringing them out of Egypt to die. The result? God sent the Israelites packing for another forty years for relying on their own assessment of the situation rather than on God's promises. Here, contrary to what church marketers imply, is a good example of the dangers of trying to determine a group's future course of action by beginning with a purely human assessment of the situation.

The Spirit of the Lord working through Caleb and Joshua apparently made it possible for them to see something that remained invisible to mere human research. They understood well that they could not take Canaan by their own savvy and strength. They also understood that God had not called them to do the best they humanly could and then expect God to pick up the slack. Rather, they understood that God was the primary actor in this drama, and so they had to ensure that they remained in God's service, and not the other way round. As a result, the children of Israel usually made sure (often at God's prompting) that they approached problems in ways that left ample room for God to remain the primary actor. This is precisely what we find lacking in the managing and marketing approach. Rather than planning in such a way that we make sure God remains the primary actor, we plan the future primarily by means of our own wisdom and then expect God to bless our efforts.

Should the Church Focus on the Measurable?

The emphasis and value that church marketers place on measurable results (primarily growth, and that defined numerically) cannot be separated from the fact that marketing is a species of management. One cannot manage what one cannot control, and in our era one cannot claim to have exercised control unless one can measure the results. It is on the basis of this principle that church marketers insist that a church's vision and goals be operationalized, or translated into measurable objectives.

Yet managing by measurable objectives will always be in tension, if not contradiction, with what the church is called to do and to be. In part, this is because most aspects of Christian growth and maturity are not quantifiable. But perhaps even more important, the overall purpose of the church cannot be operationalized. If we believe that the church is to offer an embodied witness to the truth revealed in Jesus Christ, then this leaves the church with an unachievable goal—at least in the sense that it can never be completely achieved.[23] This in itself might not be a problem, except that marketers insist that the only way we will know if we are moving toward this unachievable goal is if we first create measurable objectives that *can* be reached and then set about to reach them.[24]

One of the problems with such an approach, as anyone who has managed by objectives well knows, is that achieving these objectives begins to take on a life of its own. That is, the objectives—which begin as means to a larger end—often become ends in themselves. We see this in the church when a new set of (measurable) ends and goals is substituted for the church's God-given mission, a mission that does not lend itself to being operationalized. Educators also see this process of "substitution." They are charged with teaching the students under their care. They are told that the only "objective" way to determine whether they are being effective is to administer standardized tests. Yet once teachers know that their performance is being rated on the basis of what the test measures, teaching that particular body of information takes on an added significance. Indeed, some teachers have been known to do little more than prepare their students for these batteries of tests. Such teachers are not necessarily bad teachers or bad people, but they have found themselves caught in a system in which a means to an end has become the end itself.

Once one sees through the false dichotomy between means and ends, one begins to see that a process like marketing does not so much *serve* certain separately derived ends as it *reinforces* or *creates* certain commensurate ends. Means do impinge upon and shape ends when every marketing approach insists that the objectives must be articulated in such a way that they may be evaluated objectively—that is, quantitatively. What happens to those goals central to a church's identity and mission whose attainment cannot be specified in terms of measurable objectives? No doubt such goals will either be played down or replaced by goals whose attainment can be specified in terms of measurable objectives. Perhaps this helps to explain why church marketers avoid discussing central ecclesial concerns such as faithfulness, preferring instead to focus on growth, efficiency, and effectiveness. One cannot present a congregation with a graph that plots the church's faithfulness to its calling to be God's embodied witness in the world, but one can offer them one that plots church attendance, church contributions, and congregational satisfaction with the church's programs, and then pretend that the latter is a valid indicator of the former. Thus it seems difficult to see how a church's self-understanding and mission can resist being altered as it attempts to attain these measurable objectives. Stevens and Loudon unwittingly illustrate the way in which this transformation takes place in their discussion of how to write marketing objectives. They offer the following as an example of a poorly stated objective and how it might be improved:

Poor: Our objective is to be the best church in our area.
Remarks: Not specific enough; what measures of "best" are to be used? Attendance? Contributions? New programs started? Services offered? Number of converts?
Better: We will strive to become the number one church in the metropolitan area in terms of new converts baptized in 1989.[25]

The necessity of stating this objective in measurable terms has clearly impinged upon this church's self-understanding. Although we would agree that the original objective is lacking, we think its shortcomings have little to do with whether it's measurable; indeed, it is difficult to see how the restatement of this objective is better except that it *is* measurable. What advice would church marketers give to a congregation that had a deep desire that its life together be marked by certain theological virtues, such as love, joy, peace, patience, kindness, goodness, faithfulness, gentleness and self-control (Gal. 5:22-23)? Would they insist that the only way the congregation would ever know whether it was progressing toward its goal would be to articulate a measurable objective for each of them? And in this case, just what would measurable objectives look like?

Hence, the marketing approach imposes yet another filter through which the Christian faith must pass: A church must be able to articulate what it believes itself called to be in terms of measurable objectives; if it cannot be so articulated, then this vision must be rearticulated (re-formed) in terms of measurable objectives. In short, the marketing approach not only filters out goals that, on theological grounds, might be perfectly valid, but also substitutes its own objectives and concomitant goals.

Is Numerical Growth a Reliable Indicator of Success?

Church marketers focus on numerical growth because it lends itself to measurement and, therefore, management. If, as management theory suggests, one can demonstrate one's success at managing only what one can measure, than there is a strong impetus to focus on those aspects of church life that lend themselves to measurement. Numerical growth is one of these. Thus it is not surprising that such growth is widely considered by church marketers to be a mark of success.

Most do, of course, offer obligatory disclaimers, providing examples of well-known churches that have compromised the gospel for the sake of growth. Yet most of these disclaimers ring a bit hollow, particularly when numerical growth usually heads the list of benefits of church marketing. Of course, this should not be surprising, since this is the benefit that the business world expects to reap by effective marketing. Competing in the business world requires that a business attempt to garner an increasing share of the market. In parallel fashion, Barna insists that in order "for the local church to be a successful business, it must impact a growing share of its market area."[26] We suspect that judging success by measuring one's market share is solid business practice if you are Coca-Cola; we believe it is not a good idea for First Church at the corner of Main and Jefferson. Church marketers assume that numerical growth is a reliable indicator of success because growth is "an indication that something exciting and meaningful is happening."[27] It is interesting that this statement precedes Barna's warning about the possible intoxicating effects of growth. He seems not to see that his assumption about growth contributes to such intoxication. Lots of things grow, but growth itself is no guarantee that something "exciting and meaningful" is happening. If you are dubious, talk to someone who has had cancer. But if we rephrase Barna's sentence slightly, we might arrive at a deeper insight: "Growth *may only be* an indication that something exciting and meaningful is happening." In other words, in a society that breeds both dissatisfaction and boredom and strips us of many traditional ways of living meaningfully, the growth of a particular church may be nothing more than an indicator that it has succeeded (for the moment) in providing two existential "products" that many people intensely desire: excitement and meaning. Of course, the excitement and meaning for which the church may be a temporary vehicle may have nothing whatsoever to do with the gospel. All of this is to say that growth is an enormously unreliable indicator of faithfulness.

Jesus seems to have understood this as well. Whenever the crowds started to get large, Jesus sensed that people were misunderstanding his prophetic message and his call to costly discipleship. Indeed, Jesus made some of his starkest statements about the cost of following him when large crowds were present (see Luke 14:25-33). Before long, Jesus openly refused to meet the needs or expectations of the crowds. As a result, the multitudes went their own way. Although marketers assume that everyone in their target market can be convinced that he or she needs a certain product, Jesus understood that he was suggesting a narrow way and that "many are called but few are chosen." This means that the church should at least be circumspect when masses of people in the United States suddenly find the church attractive. Certainly, this could be the work of the Holy Spirit; but there is also the real possibility that the church has diluted the gospel in order to make it more palatable to the average consumer.

We are not suggesting that a faithful church cannot or will not grow numerically. But churches do need to recognize the enormous pressure they face to soft-pedal the gospel in order to attract and appeal to increasingly demanding and discriminating consumers. In a society obsessed with unlimited growth, and that encourages us to judge everything in terms of growth and expansion, Christians likely need to be reminded that the growth of the church is not an end in itself.[28] Indeed, though it is difficult to acknowledge in a society such as ours, neither is conversion an end in itself. Will Willimon offers a much-needed reminder:

> In a time when there is much talk of the need for more organized and scientifically managed methods of church growth, our study of the conversions in Acts raises some tough questions for proponents of many of these methods. If the church is only about the wholesale "winning of souls" by whatever method is deemed most effective, then conversion has become the end of faith rather than its beginning. . . .

Luke has no interest in the utilitarian question of *how* people become converted or *how* the church ought to evangelize, what technique is most effective or what method yields the most certain results. These are stories about *God's* actions, not the church's programs.[29]

Is Effectiveness a Reliable Indicator of Success?

Typically, one measures the success of a certain management strategy or marketing plan in terms of the values inherent in the management and marketing approach. We have already noted briefly some of the dangers of using efficiency and growth as guiding virtues. We now turn to that indicator of success most often appealed to by managers and marketers: effectiveness.

The more one reads the literature, the more one gets the feeling that "effectiveness" serves as a kind of marketing and managing mantra. Again, this should not surprise us, for as we noted earlier the manager's authority resides in his or her ability to be effective. But when church marketers make the claim that employing marketing will make the church "more effective," what exactly are they claiming?

If one presses very hard on the claims of managers and marketers to effectiveness, one soon discovers that they promise more than they can deliver. On the surface, the concept sounds very appealing. What church leader or congregation would not want to minister more effectively? But like efficiency, effectiveness does not define itself; that is, what counts for effectiveness is not self-evident. Effectiveness is always discerned with respect to some agreed upon goal or purpose. Yet marketers rarely if ever tell us what that goal or purpose is; indeed, they often make it sound as if greater effectiveness is itself the goal. At times they seem to be saying little more than, "If you adopt a marketing orientation, we'll make you more effective at being effective."[30]

127

Note how Barna insists that a church evaluate its effectiveness by polling its consumers regarding customer satisfaction. Yet such a process is dangerously circular, for in the marketing done by service industries (which Barna takes the church to be) there is no standard of effectiveness other than customer satisfaction (which presumably is measurable, at least in part, by attendance). In other words, to be an effective market-driven church is nothing other than to keep your consumers happy (and, therefore, present). This is why one group of marketers can assert that a particular congregation "is effective because it is responsive."[31] And this is why Schaller can insist that attendance is an objective measurement of "quality":

> Perhaps the most controversial question to be raised about quality, and one of the most difficult to measure, concerns that Sunday morning worship experience. In what is increasingly a consumer-driven society, the only objective measurement is attendance.[32]

So we judge whether a church's "worship experience" is effective or of high quality by measuring customer satisfaction, as measured by attendance statistics and customer surveys. But again, it is important to note that within such a scheme, the standard for effectiveness is *internal* to the marketing enterprise; an organization simply is being effective if it is keeping its customers satisfied (or "meeting their needs"). Said differently, marketing already presupposes the answer to the question, Effective at doing what? The answer is this: effective at responding to the felt needs of the consumer. But we have already suggested that there are enormous problems with conceiving of the church's identity and mission in these terms.

Yet, even if we were to grant the marketers' instrumentalist point of view, many questions about effectiveness would remain unanswered. A hammer is not effective or ineffective in the abstract; it is only so with respect to whatever task needs doing. Thus a hammer may be quite effective in driving a nail through a two-by-four, while its use may be counterproductive when it comes to replacing a transistor on your computer's circuit board.

What's bothersome about church marketers is that they think it's not their business to tell us the goals and purposes of the church. If that is the case, then they should not presume that marketing will make "almost any ministry or minister more effective."[33] We grant that marketing is effective in analyzing, planning, implementing, and controlling carefully formulated programs designed to meet the felt needs of certain target markets. What we deny is this tool's much touted universal utility; indeed, we believe that this tool should not be placed in the service of the *church's* unique mission, for to do so does serious damage to the church's self-understanding. Church marketers might be tempted to attribute our resistance to their approach to our lack of understanding about marketing; however, we think it has more to do with the way church marketers tend to misconstrue the character and mission of the church.

The church is different from the business world because effectiveness can never be the only consideration for the church. Scripture is filled with examples of people who were tempted to do (and often did) the seemingly effective thing rather than the faithful thing. Certainly, the temptations of Jesus can be understood as temptations to be effective rather than to remain faithful to his unique calling, his unique way of being the anointed of God. This is not to imply that effectiveness and faithfulness need always stand in opposition. Certainly, God can use our faithfulness as an effective witness in the world, even if this effectiveness is not easily quantifiable. But notice how this way of thinking is the inverse of the marketing approach, which places effectiveness of a certain sort in the driver's seat. As Inagrace Dietterich insists, even though the church may be concerned about faithfulness and effectiveness, it does not grant these two concerns equal status:

> The way in which the church manages itself—makes and implements decisions regarding planning, organizing, staffing, coordinating, and evaluating—is to be determined by faith commitments concerning the nature and vocation of the church. Theological understandings of the church and its calling must serve as the criteria by which the discoveries of the social sciences are critically analyzed and utilized. Thus effectiveness must be in service to faithfulness and, indeed, when considered in isolation may lead to unfaithfulness.[34]

Create Your Own Future?

We are not suggesting that the language of management is completely antithetical to the church's mission, but we do worry that it easily beguiles us into forgetting what it is we're managing. Church managers and marketers believe that they are called to be good stewards of the church. We agree with them. But certainly the first responsibility of good stewards is to make sure that when the master returns, what has been entrusted to them is still recognizable. Paul reminded the Corinthians that stewards must be faithful and trustworthy (1 Cor. 4:2). We don't think God entrusted the church to us as a service agency, so we're nervous about transforming it into one, even if doing so seems to make the church more relevant and more desirable in the eyes of the world. We believe the church has a future, but we also believe it is God's future. Rather than creating our own future, we are called to be a sign, a foretaste, and a herald of the kingdom that God is bringing. Is it possible to embrace that future kingdom without trying to manage it? In asking this, we are not suggesting that we need simply resign ourselves fatalistically to whatever future appears to be coming. But neither should we consider ourselves engineers of the future.

What would it mean to bear witness to and embody the in-breaking kingdom without trying to control the future? Perhaps a church that rightly understands its eschatological posture can take the risk of being "out of control" in this time between the times. Rather than controlling or creating the future that God alone is bringing, the church bears witness to a world that is estranged from God and that believes the future is in its own hands. Ironically, the market-driven church offers the world no real alternative by acting as if the future is in the hands of the church.

CHAPTER SEVEN

The Responsive Congregation

A S WE HAVE SEEN IN THE PREVIOUS chapters, a marketing orientation is premised upon several foundational concepts and practices, such as exchange, felt needs, segmenting, and targeting. Each of these is crucial to the marketing enterprise. However, if marketers, including church marketers, had to summarize their entire philosophy with one concept, there is little doubt what that concept would be: responsiveness.[1] Whereas in the previous discussion of targeting, responsiveness referred to the importance of targeting a segment that was likely to respond positively, here responsiveness refers more generally to the characteristic quality that market-driven churches aspire to embody.

In a nutshell, successful congregations are *responsive* religious organizations—they have structured themselves to be responsive to the needs of their current constituents, and to the needs felt by a well-defined segment of society. They are responsive by understanding what those needs are, how they might function to satisfy certain needs, the process by which persons choose a congregation to satisfy their needs, how to develop ministries and communicate the need-satisfying ability of those ministries to a specific segment, and how to

132

ensure that all this will take place within the context of a well-defined mission for the congregation. This responsiveness to internal and external needs epitomizes the essence of what a marketing orientation can contribute to religious organizations.[2]

Notice how all of this takes place "within the context of a well-defined mission." Just how does one "ensure" this will happen, given the wide-ranging character of this "responsiveness"? Isn't it likely that the church, like most businesses, will come to see its primary mission as simply being responsive? One group of church marketers seems to imply this in their lengthy treatment of responsiveness:

> The people who come in contact with these responsive congregations report high personal satisfaction. "This is the best church I ever belonged to." "This synagogue really cares about people." "This church enriches the spiritual life of all its members." These recipients (consumers) of the congregation's ministry become the best advertisement for that church or synagogue. Their goodwill and favorable word-of-mouth recommendation reach other ears and make it easy for the congregation to attract and serve more people. *The congregation is effective because it is responsive.*[3]

Here we see how effectiveness has come to be equated with responsiveness. If you ask what it is that these congregations are effective at doing, the answer is clear: effective at being responsive. But if you inquire further into why responsiveness should be the final measure of effectiveness, the answer seems to be that in a market-driven society, where consumers demand to have their needs met, no other measure counts. In a consumer-oriented culture, failing to be responsive is tantamount to failing itself.[4]

In a market-driven culture, therefore, responsiveness becomes an end in itself. In the market-driven church, responsiveness becomes the church's reason for existence. One group writes: "Religious organizations *exist* to be responsive to the needs of their members and constituents, and responsive to the needs of society. A responsive congregation is one that makes every effort to sense, serve, and satisfy the needs and wants of its members and participants within the constraints of its budget."[5]

We believe there are two primary dangers with making responsiveness the defining characteristic of a congregation. First, framing a congregation's identity in this fashion warps its view of mission. As noted above, church marketers *do* insist that all of this responsiveness should take place "within the context of a well-defined mission"; however, it appears that what makes this mission well-defined is that it is defined in terms of responsiveness. Hence, according to one group of church marketers, "from time to time, each congregation must reexamine its mission to see whether it is still on target with the needs of its members and the expectations of those it is trying to reach."[6]

What about reexamining its mission to see whether it is still on target with what God calls the church to be? Church marketers insist that what Scripture and tradition tell us about our mission should be factored into the equation, but it is only one of several considerations that must be taken into account. What must also be "held in tension" are (1) the "unique and specific needs and interests" that members want the congregation and its programs to satisfy; (2) the specific needs in the community that the congregation can and should address; and (3) the specific needs in society and the world that the congregation can and should address.[7] The notion that these things must be held in tension suggests that they are at some level at odds with each other. But what does it mean to hold in tension other concerns and what we know about the church's mission from Scripture and tradition? We believe that if the church clearly understands its mission as revealed in Scripture and tradition, then this mission ought to guide everything it does, rather than be one item among many that must be held in tension. To do anything less is to allow what *we* think the church ought to be to take precedence over what *God* desires the church to be.

Indeed, we think this is precisely what church marketing encourages, albeit unwittingly. We believe thinking about the church's mission in terms of responsiveness encourages the church to forget the big picture, to forget its reason for existence. Rather than reflecting on what kind of service our God-given mission would call us to undertake, marketing too easily assumes that serving people's needs is itself the church's mission. "A religious organization should not define its mission by listing the particular services it offers. Rather, it should identify the group(s) it wants to serve and the needs and interests of the group(s) that the organization will try to satisfy."[8]

We think this is a false choice. We don't think the church should define its mission in either of these ways, since both assume that service is an end in itself. The church does not meet needs just because it is a service agency and that's what service agencies do. Nor does the church meet certain needs because the church needs to engage in "mutually beneficial exchanges" in order to attract resources for its continued institutional existence. Both of the reasons for meeting needs and serving people misdescribe what the church is about. Both misconstrue the church's mission. The church attempts to meet certain needs in order to be responsive to *God's* call to be sign, foretaste, and herald of the kingdom. If this call is kept in view, it can serve as an important point of reference as the church engages in the hard work of discerning what kind of service it should engage in. For example, the church is called to minister to the poor, not because congregations will likely find this more inspirational than ministering to the wealthy, but because such ministry is a pointer to, as well as an embodiment of, the upside-down kingdom that God has inaugurated in Jesus Christ.[9] But this way of narrating the church's call to service is easily displaced by the alternative story of "the responsive congregation."

Too often, we forget to ask, "What is the goal of this responsiveness?" Some might say, "To attract more members to our religious organization," or "To attract more needed resources through mutually beneficial exchanges," or even, "To win more people to Christ." But such reasons are insufficient, because none of these activities is an end in itself. What is the point of these activities? Some might argue that "winning people to Christ" is an end in itself, but we believe this view to be mistaken. Election is not an end in itself. God has always been about the business of calling out a peculiar people who would by their way of life together witness to what God is doing in the world, and thereby be a "light to the nations" (Isa. 42:6; 49:6). This was Israel's calling, and it is no less the calling of the church.[10] Too often, however, both Israel and the church have taken their election as an end in itself. The goal, the purpose of this activity, is the new creation that God is bringing into being. The church stands as a pointer, a partial embodiment, an announcer of this new thing that God is doing. But the church must remember that while its task as sign, foretaste, and herald is crucial to God's reconciling and recreative work, God's design is cosmic in scope. Any understanding of the church's mission that fails to account for this grand scope is seriously deficient. This, we believe, is what is wrong with viewing the church's mission through the marketing lens of responsiveness.

There is a second, related danger with making responsiveness the defining characteristic of a congregation. By placing a premium on responsiveness and flexibility, this approach encourages the growth of "the ephemeral church," a church that simply mirrors the fleeting trends and desires of the wider society. To understand this, one must remember that the entire marketing process is a continuous one, with feedback used to evaluate and modify the church's "success."

> Because marketing is an interactive, flexible process, it has to allow for *feedback* from key sources such as dealers, agents, consumers, and competitors. The underlying concept is that the life of the product can be extended if the marketing is sensitive to market changes and consumer reactions. Once feedback is received, it needs to be processed quickly and accurately, with resulting modifications in the entire process.[11]

But once church marketers openly admit that "value is in the eye of the consumer," the practice of soliciting feedback based on customer satisfaction and customer expectation runs the risk of transforming the church into another reflection of the world's convictions. Said another way, in a consumer society renowned for its fickleness, the church that embraces flexibility and responsiveness as central principles may actually be embracing ephemerality. Church historian and theologian George Lindbeck offered sage advice about such matters a quarter century ago: "Ultimately the grounds for the Church's choices should not be guesses about 'inevitable trends' or 'waves of the future.' Rather it should be convictions about what is good and right, about what should be, rather than must be."[12] Or as Martin Marty has more recently and more pointedly observed: "To give the whole store away to match what this year's market says the unchurched want is to have the people who know least about faith determine most about its expression."[13]

Marty's comment points to how deeply proposals to market the church participate in and underwrite some of the central tenets of late modernism (what is sometimes called postmodernism).[14] Much of the emerging postmodern world focuses on style and surface, insisting that what people have traditionally called "depth" is an illusion. This emphasis on style and surface is a logical outworking of the consumer mentality. In a consumer society, people define their identities by the products they consume. But if "we are what we consume," then who we are is as ephemeral as our consumer choices. This explains why such identities are never stable or lasting and why such identities involve little more than style and surface. Said another way, people don't take their identities very seriously when they are shaped by consumption; after all, next week they may decide that they need or want something different, and so they may need to alter their lifestyles and, therefore, their identities.[15] This is why so many people believe that image is everything. An image is what is on the surface, that style or appearance that is offered for public display and consumption. In such a society, whether there is anything beneath or behind the image is all but beside the point. Products do not have images so much as images are themselves viewed as products. This helps to explain Robert Wuthnow's finding that most people who join congregational small groups do so not because they desire genuine community, which would require accountability, sacrifice, and truth telling, but because they desire the appearance, or "simulacra," of community. Such "community" demands little beyond belonging or participating, which are usually equated with "sharing one's feelings." Indeed, Wuthnow found that when such support groups *did* risk making demands on people, members often left to find another, "more supportive" group.[16]

The consumer-oriented church also mimics this emphasis on style and surface when it offers its customers different stylistic choices. For example, many churches now offer their consumers different Sunday morning options: an 8:30 worship service with a "traditional style" and an 11:00 service with a "contemporary style." The unspoken message is that the differences between services are only matters of style. Some people are into tradition; some people aren't. Some people are into contemporary music and drama; some people aren't. But there are substantive matters at stake here as well, matters that the language of "style" glosses over. If we have people in our congregations who resist singing any song or hymn that has been written in the last quarter century, offering them their own "traditional" service encourages them to believe that new expressions of devotion to God are automatically illegitimate. Such persons need to be encouraged to understand that contemporary, idiomatic expressions of faith have a place, for they remind us that this faith needs to be *our* faith. Similarly, if we are attempting to "attract" people to worship with us who neither like nor understand any song or hymn that has not been written in the last decade, offering them their own "contemporary" service encourages them to believe that they can casually dismiss more "traditional" expressions as irrelevant and outdated. These people need to be encouraged to understand that part of the power of a centuries-old hymn like "Be Thou My Vision" comes from its capacity to remind us that we stand in a long succession of saints who, in another time and place, sang this hymn. These hymns remind us that our faith is not simply "our" faith, but the faith of countless Christians across the ages. Perhaps more accurately, we see that "our" is much bigger than we might otherwise imagine.

The point, of course, is that both emphases are vital to a full understanding of the Christian faith. But rather than struggle with the difficult task of designing worship that reflects both emphases, too many churches opt for segregating their congregations according to what they (and their

139

consumers) regard as simply different "tastes" or "preferences" in worship. Here is an example in which responsiveness and customer satisfaction impede Christian formation. Both groups need to be taught the importance of something they don't like, but consumers generally aren't open to such admonition. Consumers are trained to believe that they, and they alone, are the final arbiters of what they need. Since this attitude is taken as a given in our society, it's no wonder that church marketing arrived on the scene, offering a way to exploit this mentality.

The dangers of responsiveness are subtle, for once again noble-sounding concepts (flexibility, sensitivity, service) are frequently employed. But the responsive church runs the risk of both forgetting that its mission is larger than simply being responsive to its consumers and molding itself into the fleeting image of those consumers. The church that adopts marketing techniques, with responsiveness as its guiding principle, agrees to manipulate itself until it suits a particular target audience. But given the ephemerality of the needs and desires of consumers of religion, the church that adopts such a strategy does so at great danger to its understanding of its God-given calling.

Wrong Diagnosis, Wrong Prescription

We believe that advocates of church marketing care deeply about the church and those whom the church is failing to reach. They are right to suggest that the contemporary church is sick and to insist that this sickness has serious repercussions for those inside and outside the church. We wish more people had their zeal. But as every doctor knows, zeal by itself is not enough, since zealous treatment can kill a patient if the doctor has misdiagnosed the problem. This, we believe, is the danger the contemporary church faces. One church marketer writes: "The point is clear—the

Church is not making inroads into the lives and hearts of people. *My contention, based on careful study of data and the activities of American churches, is that the major problem plaguing the Church is its failure to embrace a marketing orientation in what has become a marketing-driven environment.*"[17]

We couldn't agree more with the first statement. The church *is* failing to make an impact on the lives of many people. So we agree; the church *is* sick. But we fear that the advocates of church marketing have misdiagnosed the illness. We don't think the church is sick because it has failed "to embrace a marketing orientation in what has become a market-driven environment." We think the church is sick because it has forgotten its God-given mission to be a sign, a foretaste, and a herald of God's already-present-but-still-coming kingdom. If our diagnosis is right—if this really is what ails the church—then there is little reason to believe that the medicine the church marketers have prescribed will do any good. Indeed, there are sound reasons to believe that such medicine will do great harm.

The Marketing Prescription

Church marketers are certainly right that many people in today's society find the church "strange" in a way that earlier generations did not. This "strangeness" is widely regarded as a critical part of the church's "illness." The marketing treatment plan is premised upon three assumptions about this strangeness of the church: (1) that this strangeness is itself a problem; (2) that this strangeness is primarily a result of the church's not keeping up with the times; and (3) that the church cannot hope to evangelize an increasingly pagan society unless this strangeness is removed. These three assumptions, combined with the belief that the church service and the church building are the bridge between the wider culture and the strange culture of the church, largely shape the church-marketing treatment plan.

The unexamined assumption that the weekly worship service or the church building itself should be the centerpiece of the church's evangelism program stems from certain ways of thinking that presume a Christendom model. Within mainstream American culture, one could at one time assume a certain affinity between the culture of the church and the wider culture. In other words, one could assume a certain overlap between the language, convictions, practices, and narratives of the church and the language, convictions, practices, and narratives of the wider society. Within such a framework, evangelism often entailed little more than getting people to "come to church," for once there, much of what was happening was relatively understandable. But with the collapse of Christendom and the increasing secularization of American culture, things have changed dramatically. No longer can one assume that any overlap exists. The language, convictions, practices, and narratives of the church are all but completely alien to the unbeliever in our society. This is why many Christians today speak of the need for "pre-evangelism."

There are, however, different ways of describing this "illness," different ways of describing how and why the church has become "strange" in our day. As we have seen, marketers locate the origins of this illness in the church's insistence on being "production" and "sales" driven in a market-driven environment. With this diagnosis in hand, the marketers understandably recommend a heavy dose of marketing techniques that they believe will put the church on the road to full recovery. But there are other possible diagnoses of this "strangeness" and, therefore, other prescriptions for it. Before we point to another treatment plan, we need to summarize how the strong medicine that marketing prescribes does harm to the Body of Christ by fostering the diseased images of the church sketched in the first chapter.

Dangerous Side Effects

The marketing mentality readily assumes that the church of Jesus Christ is fundamentally like other organizations and businesses. This is why marketing language and concepts are presumed to be so easily transferable to the church's situation. But once the church is understood as a business that offers products to certain markets in order to engage in exchanges to attract resources and create profits, then everything and everyone connected with the church begins to be viewed from this perspective. The results can be devastating. Consider the new role and pressures of the pastor in this entrepreneurial church. As Barna writes, this pastor "must be a good enough businessman to keep the church solvent and make it appealing enough for people to attend before he has the chance to impact their lives."[18] How can pastors enter the pulpit each week and proclaim the truth of God's Word when they are now expected to be concerned with pleasing their customers in order to keep their congregations solvent? Can pastors and congregations really respect each other, or the place of God's Word in their midst, when their gatherings are shaped by this mentality?

In similar fashion, the marketing paradigm reconceives the church's identity and mission in terms that are "marketable." For example, church marketers cannot expect their model to function unless they can determine what the church's product is. Advocates of marketing have a tendency to identify the church's product with a congregation's programs and ministries.[19] This is true because these things lend themselves to being marketed. One of the side effects, then, of a marketing orientation is that it overemphasizes those aspects of church life that are marketable, while playing down those aspects of a church's identity and mission that are less so. How does one market a community whose purpose it is to embody an alternative way of being in the world, a community that is called to engage in such things as truth telling, forgiveness, hospitality to strangers, self-sacrifice, and love of one's enemies? Such a community does not seem marketable, because it fails to offer an attractive or desirable answer to the average person's instrumentalist question: What's it good for? Such a community is far from worthless or irrelevant, but its worth and relevance are recognized only in the light of *God's* desire for a people who will be a sign, a foretaste, and a herald of God's reconciling and re-creative work in the world.

The marketing mentality also has an adverse impact on how the church views evangelism and outreach. To see this, we need only reflect on the increasingly common use of the language of "churched" and the "unchurched."[20] As part of an evangelistic strategy, this way of speaking continues to assume that the church building is where most of the action is. Even though people who talk about the unchurched insist that building relationships with them is crucial, the goal continues to be to get them to "come to church." But once the church service or church building is viewed as one of the primary bridges to the unchurched, we have to begin asking what the service will look like through their eyes. Will they understand anything? Will they like what they do understand, at least enough to return? This is why some churches have moved to designing worship services that are "seeker-friendly" or "seeker-sensitive." As a well-known pastor has commented: "Everything we do on Sunday morning—prayers, songs, announcements—will make sense to the person walking in with no church background. So people aren't afraid to bring their friends."[21] Here we come to the crux of the issue: How much weight should a congregation place on its building and services to be the bridge for evangelism? Isn't this really the old Christendom model in different dress? Is this really "engaging the culture," as so many church marketers contend? Many of the people who adopt such a strategy appeal to the apostle Paul's willingness to "be all things to all people" (1 Cor. 9:22). But note that Paul could do this precisely because he was *out among* these different people, trying to figure out how to communicate the gospel to them in their own terms. He was not trying to figure out how to design a worship service or ministries that would attract them to a building. So perhaps we should be willing to admit that this supposedly cutting-edge approach to evangelism and outreach is still premised on the Christendom assumption that these activities take place primarily in our building on Sunday morning. But within that context, with that set of assumptions, being all things to all people breaks down.

If the church's mission is to announce the erupting reign of God, and to do so by being sign, foretaste, and herald of that kingdom, then it will not be able to do that if it expunges all its oddness in the name of building bridges to unbelievers. True, there is plenty of strangeness in the church that is an unnecessary obstacle. But we should not assume too quickly that it would automatically be a good thing if the average unbeliever understood everything that took place in our worship. One of us was a member of a Presbyterian church whose regular practice was to kneel each week for a period of personal and corporate confession. Seeing several hundred Presbyterians on their knees was a powerful reminder of our equality before God, of our utter unworthiness. Yet surely such a practice would be confusing, if not embarrassing, to a visitor. Would it be better to dispense with such practices in the name of outreach and sensitivity?

We are struck by how seldom we expect such sensitivity in other areas of our lives. What if you had never been to an opera, a hockey match, or a bar mitzvah? Would you really expect to be offered a "lite" version merely so you could be comfortable and relate to what was going on? Or would you think it is such an important activity that it's worth the work to understand what is going on, even if at first almost everything seems shrouded in mystery? These activities are rightly understood to be bigger and more important than people's discomfort at not understanding them the first time out.

Unfortunately, one of the side effects of the marketing mentality is that it clouds our thinking about the real problem with the church's strangeness. As the examples above suggest, the real problem is not the strangeness of the church; people show themselves willing to wrestle with strangeness all the time. *The real problem is that unbelievers have so few reasons to endure the church's strangeness.* People usually are led to endure their first uncomfortable trips to the opera or a hockey game because they know people who cannot imagine what their lives would be like without them. They go to see what all the fuss is about. But for the average unbeliever in this country, there is no fuss to wonder about. They live, work, and play alongside Christians every day and can see virtually no difference that any of this makes. So why endure the strangeness when it is so obvious that none of it makes the least bit of difference in how people live? Viewed from this angle, the marketing approach *does* have the advantage of being more honest. Since the church so rarely lives any differently from the world, the church should stop erecting artificial barriers that put people off. After all, it's hard to justify designing worship services that seem strange to unbelievers when nothing we do the rest of the week seems the least bit strange to them.

But there is another way in which the marketing medicine is designed to alleviate the strangeness of the church. Since to the unbeliever the Body of Christ only appears to be strange on Sunday mornings, marketing techniques encourage us to reach out to the unchurched and show them that we aren't really strange at all. Some churches do this by offering "church lite," by offering worship services that are in no way strange. Even more bothersome are the ways in which marketing encourages the church to reach out to the unchurched by offering them instrumentalist reasons to justify their participation. Church marketers assume that the only persuasion that can take place is persuasion that has self-interested exchanges at the center. As a result, the marketing prescription encourages us to reach out to our unbelieving neighbors and persuade them that the church is actually what they're already looking for and desire. We are relevant; we can meet their self-determined needs.

Such medicine harms the church by giving it selective memory. We offer our neighbors the good news of salvation, but forget to tell them the seemingly bad news about repentance and conversion. In other words, we market salvation (which is marketable, because it does have "instrumental" value) and fail to proclaim that God requires us to repent, to turn away from our former ways of thinking and acting—which ultimately lead to death. This part of the good news is harder to market, and no less easier for the church to embody. Yet the church is called to be engaged in a persuasive activity whose logic differs from what characterizes the relevant, self-interested, full-service, therapeutic, ephemeral church. Rather than insisting, with the instrumentalist church, that the Body of Christ really is what they're looking for, that it (already) speaks to the desires of our unbelieving neighbors, the church of Jesus Christ is called to proclaim and embody to those neighbors that God is (already) looking for and desiring them.

Such a suggestion shows how little room there is for God to act in the marketing approach. Perhaps more accurately, it shows how little need there is for God to act. The marketing approach makes the work of the Spirit redundant, if not unnecessary, for this strategy encourages us to think of conversion as rooted in human calculation. What is most dangerous about this aspect of the marketing medicine is that it works. That is, there are people who can be made to feel better about themselves and their lives by being encouraged to view their relationship to the church as another consumer choice. But in a society like ours, where everything is in danger of being reduced to a preference or a lifestyle choice, congregations must consider carefully whether they should do anything to encourage people to view the church in this manner. As Hauerwas and Willimon warn, in a society steeped in individualism and its resulting loneliness, offering people "community" as a lifestyle choice will often be viewed as attractive, but such communities may have little or nothing to do with the gospel.

> When people are very detached, very devoid of purpose and a coherent world view, Christians must be very suspicious of talk about community. In a world like ours, people will be attracted to communities that promise them an easy way out of loneliness, togetherness based on common tastes, racial or ethnic traits, or mutual self-interest. There is then little check on community becoming as tyrannical as the individual ego. Community becomes totalitarian when its only purpose is to foster a sense of belonging in order to overcome the fragility of the lone individual. Christian community, life in the colony, is not primarily about togetherness. It is about the way of Jesus Christ with those whom he calls to himself. It is about disciplining our wants and needs in congruence with a true story, which gives us the resources to lead truthful lives. In living out the story together, togetherness happens, but only as a by-product of the main project of trying to be faithful to Jesus.[22]

In other words, the church marketing medicine does not require the Spirit for it to be "effective." There is no need for the Spirit to empower us to die to self. Indeed, we don't plan to die to self at all; we're in this to improve or enrich our "selves." Said another way, the engineered church is the church for atheists. As William Willimon has rightly argued, "atheism is the conviction that the presence and power of God are unessential to the work of ministry, that we can find the right technique, the proper approach, and the appropriate attitude and therefore will not need God to validate our ministry."[23]

We have already noted that one group of marketers has argued that "wrong thinking consists of planning the ministry—and then trying to convince the target group that it really is best for them."[24] But maybe our job is not primarily the one of convincing people that the ministry we have planned for them really is best for them; maybe our job is one of living faithfully before the world and allowing God to use our embodied testimony to bring about conversion. Perhaps evangelism is not about serving people's felt needs as a way of securing an audience, but about living in a way that demands conversion to be understood. Jesus seems to have gone about his ministry in ways that required the Spirit to be active if people were to understand what he was about. Contrary to popular belief, Jesus did not instruct in parables because he was trying to make things easy and accessible; if that had been his goal and motivation, then he was a terrible failure, as witnessed by the countless times he had to explain himself to even his closest associates.

We have already suggested that one of the common side effects of the marketing medicine is selective memory. But there is also the danger that this medicine might induce complete forgetfulness. It is possible that viewing the church through the marketing perspective might lead to a complete loss of memory, to a complete loss of perspective concerning what the church is about in the first place. If this occurred, it would not be the first time it had happened to God's people, though it would not be any less serious a side effect. Walter Brueggemann, commenting on Israel's amnesia, notes their response to their forgetfulness once they had been shown their waywardness:

> In the disciplines of fasting and sackcloth, the Israelites "separated themselves from all foreigners" and confessed their sin (Neh 9:1-2). This act in the drama needs to be understood carefully. Wrongly understood, according to Christian stereotypes of Jews, this separation sounds like arrogant legalism. Such a view misses the point completely. Rather, this community in its amnesia had assimilated itself, domesticated its memory, and compromised its identity, so that it had nothing left of itself. Judaism had become such a detrimental embarrassment, that Jews had worked to overcome their Jewishness. And now, in these dangerous liturgical acts, Jews are facing up to their oddity, to their strong commitment, to their distinctive obedience. The recovery of distinctiveness entails the acceptance of an odd identity. I report this point to you because I believe the church in the United States faces a crisis of accommodation and compromise that is near to final evaporation. Note well, the distinctiveness is not in doctrine or in morality, but in memory. For the text adds that all through this time of separation, "They stood up in their place and read from the book of the law." (9:3)[25]

Finally, one of the side effects of the marketing treatment plan is that it encourages the development of homogeneous communities. Again, many marketing advocates suggest that this is no side effect at all. Indeed, Lyle Schaller has suggested that the argument between those who would consciously or unconsciously create homogeneous communities and those who believe such communities are an affront to the gospel is really little more than an argument between those people animated by pragmatism and those animated by ideology.[26] We don't think this side effect can be rendered harmless as easily as that. We believe the indictment that Padilla brings against church growth missiology, with its willingness to make use of the homogeneous unit principle, is equally applicable to church marketing:

> Because of its failure to take biblical theology seriously, it has become a missiology tailor-made for churches and institutions whose main function in society is to reinforce the status quo. What can this missiology say to a church in an American suburb, where the bourgeois is comfortable but remains enslaved to the materialism of a consumer society and blind to the needs of the poor? What can it say to a church where a racist "feels at home" because of the unholy alliance of Christianity with racial segregation? What can it say in situations of tribal, caste, or class conflict? Of course, it can say that "men like to become Christians without crossing racial, linguistic and class barriers." But what does that have to do with the gospel concerning Jesus Christ, who came to reconcile us "to God *in one body* through the cross"?[27]

It's difficult to see how the homogeneous church can be a sign, a foretaste, and a herald of anything other than the social arrangements people naturally embody. God need not be involved in the building of the homogeneous church; we can build this church on our own. We are reminded that Peter urges us to consider ourselves as "living stones" that are being "built into a spiritual house" (1 Pet. 2:5). Too many churches look like "spiritual houses" that have been constructed out of identical bricks or cinder blocks. Such structures would certainly be stronger if mortar held them together, but the bricks or blocks, by virtue of their similarity, are capable of standing for awhile simply by being stacked one on top of one another. We believe that God desires to build a spiritual house that more closely resembles a river-rock church, a structure whose every stone is a different size, shape, and color. These buildings are a powerful testimony to God's involvement, for it is only by the adhesive of God's Spirit that such structures are held together.

By now it should be obvious that many of the challenges church marketing raises for the church are not new ones. Many of the difficult questions revolve around the ways humans are called to cooperate in God's economy of salvation to bring about God's purposes. Church marketers insist that they are merely being pragmatic, merely using the resources that God has placed at their disposal as a means to minister more effectively.

> [The critics of church marketing] may not realize that God has called us to behave intelligently, using the means and resources he has provided to accomplish his ends. Many of our critics will fail to realize that the marketing process itself is neither holy nor unholy; it is how we use and perceive the process, and the fruits of the process, that determine whether or not we have abused it. If we put all our trust in our own marketing abilities, or if our marketing efforts are successful in reaching people for the Church, and we give all the credit to the marketing process rather than to God's blessing on our efforts, only then are our critics correct.[28]

The problem, of course, is that the Bible is replete with examples of God urging people to set aside available resources and the "reasonable" way of doing things in order to demonstrate their trust in God, in order to allow God room to act decisively. Gideon is commanded to send home all but 300 of his 32,000 soldiers so that all will know that God, not Gideon and his army, has defeated the Midianites (Judges 7). When the young man David goes out to meet mighty Goliath, he leaves behind the available resources of warfare, knowing that God is the one who will deliver him (1 Samuel 17). And Jesus resists temptation throughout his ministry, including his time on the cross, to use the power that is available to him for purposes he discerns are incompatible with the new kingdom he is establishing. Wouldn't using his "available resources" to come down from the cross—silencing his skeptics and demonstrating for all the world his true identity—be a reasonable and fitting way to usher in the new kingdom? (See Matt. 27:42).

The assumption among church marketers seems to be that if a resource is available, it must be from God. And if God has given us this resource, we are thereby warranted to use it to accomplish God's purposes, so long as we remember to give God the credit for blessing our efforts when we "succeed." The church marketers are not the first in church history to make such an assumption. In the fourth century, Augustine believed that God's providence was responsible for Constantine's embracing Christianity, thereby placing the reigns of power in the hands of Christians for the first time. Augustine thought this meant the church was now justified in using its newfound power to coerce wayward Christians back into the fold. In retrospect, many think Augustine was mistaken. Similar assumptions were no doubt held by many Crusaders, who thought they were merely using the resources that God had given them, such as the sword and the power of the medieval monarchy, to convert the masses to Christ. In retrospect, many also think the Crusaders were mistaken. Finally, many Christians in the United States believe their country fully justified in exploding nuclear weapons over Hiroshima and Nagasaki, not least because they believe God provided these resources. Again, many believe these Christians are wrong. Too often, it seems, the church has been tempted to believe that this new kingdom God is bringing could be established by using the methods of the old kingdom that is passing away. But part of what makes this new kingdom *new* is that it is rooted in a new reality, a new social order, a new way of doing things.

Karl Barth noted that the church has always been tempted to bridge the gap between the church and the world by becoming more like the world. But when the church adopts this strategy, it loses its very reason for being, its very reason for reaching out to the world, which is to offer the world an embodied alternative to being the world. If the church is called to be a sign, a foretaste, and a herald of the new kingdom God has established in Christ, then it cannot hope to be faithful to that calling by being more like the old kingdom that is passing away. Barth's warning is worth quoting at length.

It will usually be argued that it is a question of mediation, of bridging the gap between those outside and those inside, of works of "sincerity" on the one side and serious and necessary attempts to win the world for Christ on the other; or that it is a question of the translation of the Christian into the secular at the command of love; or conversely of a translation of the secular into the Christian, of a kind of baptism of non-Christian ideas and customs and enterprises by new Christian interpretations and the giving of a new Christian content, or of a minting of Christian gold on behalf of poor non-Christians. And it is all very fine and good so long as there is no secret respect for the fashion of the world, no secret listening to its basic theme, no secret hankering after its glory; and, conversely, no secret fear that the community cannot live solely by Jesus Christ and the free grace of God, no secret unwillingness to venture to allow itself to live and grow simply from its own and not a worldly root as the *communio sanctorum* [communion of saints] in the world (not against the world but for it, not in conflict but in what is, rightly considered, the most profound peace with it). Where there is this respect, this listening, this hankering, this fear and unwillingness, it always means the secularisation of the community. Secularisation is the process at the end of which it will be only a part of the world among so much else of the world; one of the religious corners which the world may regard as necessary to its fulness but which do not have the slightest practical significance for its manner and way. Secularisation is the process by which the salt loses it savour (Matt 5:13). It is not in any sense strange that the world is secular. This is simply to say that the world is the world. It was always secular. There is no greater error than to imagine that this was not the case in the much-vaunted Middle Ages. But when the Church becomes secular, it is the greatest conceivable misfortune both for the Church and the world. . . . It then loses its specific importance and meaning; the justification for its existence.[29]

A Different Prescription: An Embodied Question Mark

Our goal in this book has not been to offer and justify a completely different treatment plan. Although this task remains to be done and is badly needed, our goal here has been more modest: to give sound reasons for believing that the marketing medicine is injurious to the long-term health of the church. We hope our critique to this point has hinted at the type of medicine we would prescribe for the church, given our diagnosis of the church's illness. All we can do in the space remaining is to make a few additional suggestions that we hope will spark the imaginations of faithful Christians everywhere who care about the future of the church.

We would be the first to admit that part of the attraction of church marketing is that it seems to offer a relatively quick remedy for a serious illness. Ministers often feel enormous pressure to come up with quick fixes for congregations suffering from declining attendance, offerings, and commitment. As one of our friends has pointedly asked: "This critique of the marketing mentality may be well and good, but what do you have to put in its place? What do I say to my board?"

Although we want to resist the purely pragmatic temptation to offer different "how-to" advice, we don't thereby want to imply that there is nothing the church or its leaders can do. For example, one important thing congregations can do is to make a commitment to struggle diligently against the market logic that not only surrounds the congregations, but also is likely present in the congregation already, even if it has never recognized it before. Granted, this is not currently the major cause of illness for many churches, but it does sap the church's vital energies by directing them toward activities that only threaten the church's long-term health. While we might be tempted to minimize the importance of such a commitment, we should never think it a small matter when a doctor chooses to take us off a certain medication because the doctor is convinced that it is making us sicker.

Such a commitment, however, is not enough. We want the doctor to go on to determine *why* the medicine was making us sicker rather than better. Are we simply allergic to this medication, or has the doctor misdiagnosed our illness (or both)? With respect to church marketing, the answer seems to be that both things are the case. There are good reasons to think that the Body of Christ is allergic to the marketing mentality, and there are good reasons to believe that church marketers have misdiagnosed the church's illness. But what really ails the church? What kind of medicine might begin to bring restoration?

We have argued throughout this book that the church is plagued by a loss of memory. It has forgotten why God has called it into being. It has forgotten that God has called it to be a sign, a foretaste, and a herald of God's new creation. What it needs most, therefore, is a new and powerful vision of what God has called it to be in the world. We think that René Padilla has offered just such a powerful vision: "The missiology that the church needs today is not one that conceives the people of God as a *quotation* taken from the surrounding society, but one that conceives it as an *'embodied question-mark'* that challenges the values of the world."[30]

This is precisely the vision that the contemporary church most needs: a renewed sense that God has called it to be, not a quotation from the surrounding society, but an embodied question mark. Can the church conduct itself in such a way that its embodied life together calls into question the ways of the world, rather than mimicking them? We believe that God can use this vision of the church to call it back to what God called it to be. We believe it has enormous possibilities for energizing the imaginations of Christians who desire to be faithful to God's call to be a sign, a foretaste, and a herald of the kingdom. We don't pretend to know all the ramifications of such a vision for the everyday life of the church, but we are excited to think about the possibilities that congregations might be led to consider. We offer a couple of modest suggestions as a way of starting this important conversation and exploration.

We think the church might do well to bring back some form of catechesis. In our society, the church needs a practice that signals the seriousness of following the way of God. The church needs a way to let people know up front what some of the costs of following Jesus Christ are. (We need to remember that this is the context—costly discipleship—in which Jesus encourages his listeners to "count the cost"; ironically, church marketers often imply that Jesus issued this directive as a way of promoting a general principle regarding planning.) In other words, if the church is called to be an embodied question mark, if what it means to be a member of the Body of Christ is not "natural," then the church will need a new emphasis on the formation of Christian character (an emphasis that is likely more attuned to "production" language than to "consumer" images).[31] But such formation must be tied to ecclesiology. Instead of being a place for the consumption of different religious experiences, the church should understand itself as a crucible for forming people capable of embodying their calling to be a sign, a foretaste, and a herald of the kingdom. This would mean that as a community we would be more concerned about the way our character is being formed than we would about whether a certain style of worship is in line with our consumer tastes and preferences. In other words, we would be encouraged to think of our identities in terms of who we were becoming instead of in terms of the religious products we were consuming.[32]

We also think that pastors and their congregations would do well to rethink the way they conceive of preaching. Too often, preaching has been stripped of its ability to embody our belief that God is speaking through the preached word. Too often pastors and congregations act as if this activity is merely another form of human communication that we hope God will use. But if this gathering is like no other human gathering, if this preaching moment is like no other form of human communication, then perhaps we should preach (and listen) as if something different is going on. Perhaps the church that views itself as an embodied question mark will see the wisdom, as Willimon suggests, of preaching as if a miracle will be needed for it to be heard and understood.

Desiring too desperately to communicate, at any cost, can lead us into apostasy. The odd way in which God has saved us presents a never-ending challenge to those who are called to talk about it. . . . Can we preachers respect the gospel enough to allow people not to understand it? We are not responsible for all failures of communication. The gospel itself, in collision with the corruptions engendered by life in a democratic, capitalist society, bears some of the responsibility for people not hearing. We preachers so want to be heard that we are willing to make the gospel more accessible than it really is, to remove the scandal, the offense of the cross, to deceive people into thinking that it is possible to hear without conversion. This is the great lie behind most of my apologetics, the deceit that it is possible to hear the gospel while we are still trapped in outmoded or culturally conditioned patterns of thought and hearing. How are we extricated from such patterns? Only by being confronted by the gospel. How does the gospel manage to work such power among epistemologically enslaved folk like us? I don't know. It's a miracle. . . . We must learn to preach again in such a way as to demonstrate that, if there is no Holy Spirit, if Jesus has not been raised from the dead, then our preaching is doomed to fall upon deaf ears. Our preaching ought to be so confrontive, so in violation of all that contemporary Americans think they know, that it requires no less than a miracle to be heard. We preach best with a reckless confidence in the power of the gospel to evoke the audience it deserves.[33]

Like most of the life of the church, these two activities, formation and preaching, should not be thought of as distinct practices. They are deeply connected. Willimon makes this clear when in another context he writes: "When I was in seminary, someone told us in preaching class that the gospel must be translated into the thought forms of the modern world or we would not be heard. The preacher is the bridge between the world of the Bible and the world of the twentieth century. I've decided that the traffic has been moving in only one direction on that bridge. Our task as preachers is not the hermeneutical one of making the gospel capable of being heard by modern people but the pastoral-political job of making a people who are capable of hearing the gospel."[34]

159

The Responsive Congregation

One of the many ironies of church marketing is that it doesn't seem to apply its principles to itself. Marketing is marketed as a product for every organization. But adopting such a strategy makes sense only if a group already understands itself (or is willing to begin understanding itself) primarily in those terms that shape relationships within market economies. What if congregations refuse to view themselves in such terms? Shouldn't marketers, of all people, be willing to admit that there are some groups of people who neither need nor want their product? No one denies that marketing occupies a huge niche in the overall structure of American society. Yet why must its advocates insist that every organization, including the church, would be better off if it viewed itself and the rest of the world through the spectacles of marketing?[35]

Ultimately, we don't believe the issue is *whether* the church will be responsive, but *how* the church will be so. Said another way, the issue is not whether the church will engage the wider culture, but how it will engage it. The church most effectively engages the wider culture, not when it strives to be more like it in order to gain a hearing, but when it strives to be responsive to God's calling for it to be a sign, a foretaste, and a herald of God's work in the world. We offer unbelievers little, except perhaps more and better reasons to persist in their unbelief, when they see little that distinguishes the people of God from the rest of the world. What would happen if unbelievers looking at the Body of Christ were given the opportunity to see not a pale reflection of themselves, but an embodied question mark?

The Man Nobody Knows

For we are God's servants, working together; you are God's field, God's building. According to the grace of God given to me, like a skilled master builder I laid a foundation, and someone else is building on it. Each builder must choose with care how to build on it. For no one can lay any foundation other than the one that has been laid; that foundation is Jesus Christ. Now if anyone builds on the foundation with gold, silver, precious stones, wood, hay, straw—the work of each builder will become visible, for the Day will disclose it, because it will be revealed with fire, and the fire will test what sort of work each has done. (1 Cor. 3:9-13)

IN HIS FIRST LETTER TO THE CORINTHIANS, the apostle Paul warns those who are responsible for "building" the church of Christ. Some Christians in Corinth had become enamored of certain forms of "wisdom" and with those who had instructed them in this wisdom. Apparently, some had even begun to ridicule Paul for preaching such a simple gospel (1 Cor. 2:1-2). Paul responds by reminding the Corinthians that the responsibility for building the church is an awesome one. "Do you not know that you are God's temple and that God's Spirit dwells in you? If anyone destroys God's temple, God will destroy that person. For God's temple is holy, and you are that temple" (1 Cor. 3:16-17).

According to Paul, the foundation for this new building project has already been laid. This foundation is Jesus Christ. Therefore, their task as builders was to build upon that foundation, using materials that would withstand the test of the final judgment. What will last are those materials compatible with the foundation: Jesus Christ and the gospel of him crucified. What will perish are those materials incompatible with the foundation because they are constructed from merely human wisdom. For this reason, Paul goes on to warn the Corinthians: "If you think that you are wise in this age, you should become fools so that you may become wise. For the wisdom of this world is foolishness with God" (1 Cor. 3:18-19).

Paul's warning to the church at Corinth shows that he believed two important things about the church. First, this "building" is unique. The church is like no other community: Its foundation is Jesus Christ and him crucified, and God's Spirit dwells within its members corporately. There are many groups of people in the world; there are many different communities. But this community of the crucified Jesus is the dwelling place of God's Spirit in a way like no other. Second, and no less important to Paul, this building is like no other because it is built by different means, means that reflect the character of the foundation itself. Paul insists that he didn't peddle the gospel to the Corinthians by proclaiming lofty words of wisdom; rather, he came in weakness, proclaiming "the foolishness of God," so that their faith would rest not in worldly wisdom but in the power of God (1 Cor. 2:1-5). As Gordon Fee suggests, Paul's warning to the Corinthians needs to be heard again in our day:

> It is unfortunately possible for people to attempt to build the church out of every imaginable human system predicated on merely worldly wisdom, be it philosophy, "pop" psychology, managerial techniques, relational "good feelings," or what have you. But at the final judgment, all such building (and perhaps countless other forms, where systems have become more important than the gospel itself) will be shown for what it is: something merely human, with no character of Christ or his gospel in it. Often, of course, the test may come this side of the final one, and in such an hour of stress that which has been built of modern forms of *sophia* usually comes tumbling down.[1]

Some advocates of marketing might counter our criticisms and warnings by pointing to the spiritual growth that has been achieved, at least in part, as a result of their marketing efforts. We do not want to deny that God is capable of working through any means God desires. And God certainly seems in the past to have "redeemed" even less noble means than marketing techniques. Yet acknowledging that God is capable of using even our failures and our unfaithfulness to God's own purposes can never warrant our encouraging fellow Christians to think and act in ways that we have good reasons to believe are at cross-purposes with God's kingdom (Rom. 6:1-2). God's ability to work through even the unlikeliest of avenues should not be taken as a license to commend to God's people ways of conceiving of the church's identity and mission in ways that will likely impede the Spirit's work. We're confident that advocates of church marketing would agree that we are called to participate with, not against, God in the ministry of reconciliation (2 Cor. 5:18-19). Where we differ is that marketers clearly believe that using marketing techniques is an appropriate way to cooperate with God in such work; in contrast, we are convinced that the theological assumptions of such techniques are at cross-purposes with God's ministry of reconciliation.

We believe that the gospel of Jesus Christ—the good news that calls us to die to self—is being supplanted by a new "gospel of consumer orientation."[2] Can we really build on the foundation that has already been laid with this new "good news"? Perhaps only the final judgment will reveal definitively whether this new gospel amounts to more than "wood, hay, and straw." Nevertheless, we do not think it premature to ask our brothers and sisters in Christ to examine carefully the materials and methods they are using to build the church of Christ. Such examination is never easy, for in asking hard questions we always risk offending those whom we think well-intentioned but misguided. Yet such examination is necessary if the church is to remain faithful to its calling to be a sign, a foretaste, and a herald of God's kingdom.

Earlier in this century, Bruce Barton wrote an enormously popular book entitled *The Man Nobody Knows.*[3] The premise of this book is that the Scriptures reveal a Jesus whom people failed to acknowledge. Jesus, says Barton, was a man who was arguably the best "salesman" the world has ever known. If we would just study Jesus' selling techniques, we would be well on our way to becoming successful salesmen ourselves. Barton, like the advocates of church marketing after him, was convinced that Scripture offers us wisdom and techniques that at some level we already know and desire. In our day, the "man nobody knows" is not Barton's Jesus, the salesman (or marketer?) who has been created in our own image. Rather, it is the Jesus who reveals to us something we neither know nor desire apart from him: that the way to life is through death.

NOTES

1. The Frog in the Kettle

1. George Barna, *A Step-by-Step Guide to Church Marketing: Breaking Ground for the Harvest* (Ventura, Calif.: Regal Books, 1992), p. 14.
2. Serious theological critiques of church marketing are relatively rare, but we are certainly not the first to raise some of these issues. See, for example, Douglas D. Webster, *Selling Jesus* (Inter-Varsity Press, 1992); Marva J. Dawn, *Reaching Out Without Dumbing Down: A Theology of Worship for the Turn-of-the-Century Culture* (Grand Rapids: Eerdmans, 1995); and David Wells, *God in the Wasteland* (Grand Rapids: Eerdmans, 1994), esp. pp. 60-87. Several of the ideas in the following pages were first developed by Kenneson in his article "Selling [Out] the Church in the Marketplace of Desire," *Modern Theology* 9 (October 1993): 319-48.
3. Norman Shawchuck, Philip Kotler, Bruce Wrenn, and Gustave Rath, *Marketing for Congregations: Choosing to Serve People More Effectively* (Nashville: Abingdon Press, 1992), p. 31. The authors borrow the phrase "religious museums" from Gary A. Tobin, Professor of Modern Jewish Studies at Brandeis University.
4. Ibid., p. 136.
5. For the classic, and in many ways prophetic, statement of this thesis, see Philip Rieff, *The Triumph of the Therapeutic* (Chicago: University of Chicago Press, 1967).
6. See Robert Wuthnow, *Sharing the Journey: Support Groups and America's New Quest for Community* (New York: The Free Press, 1994).
7. Note, for example, the subtitle of Shawchuck, Kotler, Wrenn, and Rath, *Marketing for Congregations: Choosing to Serve People More Effectively*.
8. George Barna, *The Frog in the Kettle: What Christians Need to Know About Life in the Year 2000* (Ventura, Calif.: Regal Books, 1990), p. 227.

2. Dying for Change

1. Robert E. Stevens and David L. Loudon, *Marketing for Churches and Ministries* (New York: Haworth Press, 1992), p. 3.

2. Norman Shawchuck, Philip Kotler, Bruce Wrenn, and Gustave Rath, *Marketing for Congregations: Choosing to Serve People More Effectively* (Nashville: Abingdon Press, 1992), p. 43.
3. Lyle E. Schaller, *Create Your Own Future!* (Nashville: Abingdon Press, 1991), p. 133.
4. Stevens and Loudon, *Marketing for Churches and Ministries*, p. ix; italics added.
5. George Barna, *Marketing the Church* (Colorado Springs, Colo.: NavPress, 1988), p. 56.
6. George Barna, *A Step-by-Step Guide to Church Marketing: Breaking Ground for the Harvest* (Ventura, Calif.: Regal Books, 1992), p. 28.
7. Leith Anderson, *Dying for Change* (Minneapolis: Bethany House Publishers, 1990).

3. Marketing the Church

1. "AMA Board Approves New Marketing Definition," *Marketing News* (March 1, 1985): 1, as quoted in Louis E. Boone and David L. Kurtz, *Contemporary Marketing*, 7th ed. (Fort Worth: Dryden Press, 1992), p. 6. The following account of marketing's distinctiveness follows closely Boone and Kurtz.
2. This periodization of "eras" was first articulated by Theodore Levitt in his influential book, *Innovations in Marketing* (New York: McGraw-Hill, 1962). For an example of the way this story is assumed in marketing textbooks, see Boone and Kurtz, *Contemporary Marketing*, pp. 7-13.
3. Robert J. Keith, "The Marketing Revolution," *Journal of Marketing* (January 1960): 36.
4. Boone and Kurtz, *Contemporary Marketing*, p. 8.
5. Keith, "The Marketing Revolution," p. 38.
6. Ibid. Many marketers date the beginning of this marketing revolution to 1952, when General Electric announced in its annual report that it was adopting a new management philosophy that was consumer oriented: "[The concept] introduces the [marketer] at the beginning rather than at the end of the production cycle and integrates marketing into each phase of the business. Thus, marketing, through its studies and research, will establish for the engineer, the design and manufacturing [person], what the customer wants in a given product, what price he [or she] is willing to pay, and where and when it will be wanted. Marketing will have authority in product planning, production scheduling, and inventory control, as well as in sales, distribution, and servicing of the product" (General Electric Company, *Annual Report* [1952]: 21, as quoted in Boone and Kurtz, *Contemporary Marketing*, p. 11).
7. This is a central thesis of R. Laurence Moore's study, *Selling God: American Religion in the Marketplace of Culture* (New York: Oxford University Press, 1994). See also Nathan O. Hatch, *The Democratization of American Christianity* (New Haven, Conn.: Yale University Press, 1989).
8. See Richard M. Titmuss, *The Gift Relationship: From Human Blood to Social Policy* (New York: Pantheon Books, 1971), and Andrew Kimbrell, *The Human Body Shop: The Engineering and Marketing of Life* (San Francisco: HarperSanFrancisco, 1993), esp. pp. 6-23.
9. George Barna, *Marketing the Church* (Colorado Springs, Colo.: NavPress, 1988), p. 29.

10. George Barna, *A Step-by-Step Guide to Church Marketing: Breaking Ground for the Harvest* (Ventura, Calif.: Regal Books, 1992), pp. 14-15. This quotation is Barna's telling response to the mixed reception of his early book on church marketing theory, *Marketing the Church*; italics added.
11. Norman Shawchuck, Philip Kotler, Bruce Wrenn, and Gustave Rath, *Marketing for Congregations: Choosing to Serve People More Effectively* (Nashville: Abingdon Press, 1992), p. 21; italics added.
12. Barna, *Marketing the Church*, pp. 26-27; italics added.
13. Ibid., p. 23; italics added.
14. Interview with George Barna, *Leadership* (Summer 1995): 123; italics added.
15. Barna, *Marketing the Church*, p. 16.
16. Shawchuck, Kotler, Wrenn, and Rath, *Marketing for Congregations*, p. 43.
17. Barna, *Marketing the Church*, p. 33.
18. Ibid., p. 41.
19. Shawchuck, Kotler, Wrenn, and Rath, *Marketing for Congregations*, p. 22.
20. Ibid., p. 19.
21. Ibid., pp. 57-64.
22. We refer to the marketers' curious use of Scripture at several points throughout our argument. One particular example of special pleading is Barna's discussion of Jesus as marketing researcher: "If you review Jesus' ministry, you will discover many examples of His mastery of the data gathering and analysis process. Jesus consciously sought to identify people's needs—not by making gross assumptions, but through research (either by questioning the individual, or through keen observation). He asked the blind man what he wanted. He asked the centurion what he desired. At the Cana wedding, His conversation with Mary uncovered the need for more wine" (*Marketing the Church*, pp. 30-31).
23. Boone and Kurtz, *Contemporary Marketing*, p. 7.
24. Irenaeus *Against Heresies* 4.25, as quoted in Thomas Spidlik, *Drinking from the Hidden Fountain: A Patristic Breviary* (Kalamazoo, Mich.: Cistercian Publications, 1993), p. 27.
25. It is interesting that several well-known economists recognize the important place of gifts in any contemporary economy, yet church marketers are all but silent on this matter. Indeed, one group of marketers argues that "marketing organizations rely on exchange mechanisms, rather than threat systems, on the one hand, or love systems on the other, to achieve their goals" (Shawchuck, Kotler, Wrenn, and Rath, *Marketing for Congregations*, p. 45). This reference to "threat" and "love" systems is to the work of economist Kenneth E. Boulding, who argues that exchange systems alone do not adequately describe the motivations underlying most economies, since almost all economies also involve the issuing of threats and the giving of gifts. See, for example, his *The Economy of Love and Fear* (Belmont, Calif.: Wadsworth Publishing, 1973). We wish that this group of church marketers, who acknowledge Boulding's work, had clarified so central a theological concept as "gift." But even in their section on fund raising, they insist that "giving" be understood as an exchange: "The main point is that the congregation must view the act of receiving money from an individual donor as an exchange—and the more clergy and lay leaders understand the motives for giving, the more capable they become of ensuring that the 'something-of-value' will be received by the donor in exchange for the con-

167

tribution." See Shawchuck, Kotler, Wrenn, and Rath, *Marketing for Congregations*, pp. 357-58.

26. Martin Luther, "The Freedom of a Christian," in *Martin Luther: Selections from His Writings*, ed. John Dillenberger (Garden City, N.Y.: Anchor Books, 1961), pp. 60-61.

27. Augustine *On Psalm 33*, 9, as quoted in Spidlik, *Drinking from the Hidden Fountain*, p. 369.

28. Karl Barth, *The Epistle to the Romans*, trans. Edwyn C. Hoskyns (Oxford: Oxford University Press, 1968), p. 423.

29. Maximus the Confessor *Centuries on Charity* 3.56, as quoted in Spidlik, *Drinking from the Hidden Fountain*, p. 223.

30. Luther, "The Freedom of a Christian," pp. 74, 75-76.

31. Thomas Murray, "Gifts of the Body and the Needs of Strangers," *Hastings Center Report* (April 1987): 31.

32. What makes this exchange "abstract" is that what is actually being exchanged is largely absent. Your currency, which you are exchanging for the cereal, actually represents the time and labor that you have exchanged for that currency. The box of cereal, in turn, represents the time and effort of countless people, only one of whom (the check-out clerk, the person most removed from the actual production of the cereal) is actually present at the point of exchange.

33. Max Weber, *Economy and Society*, vol. 2, ed. Guenther Roth and Claus Witich (New York: Bedminster Press, 1968), p. 636.

34. Barna, *A Step-by-Step Guide to Church Marketing*, p. 21.

35. Karl Barth, as quoted in David F. Wells, *God in the Wasteland* (Grand Rapids: Eerdmans, 1994), p. 60.

4. User-Friendly Churches

1. Norman Shawchuck, Philip Kotler, Bruce Wrenn, and Gustave Rath, *Marketing for Congregations: Choosing to Serve People More Effectively* (Nashville: Abingdon Press, 1992), p. 57. Instead of this tripartite division, Barna often appeals to the distinction between product-driven and market-driven organizations. For example, he writes: "If you study how organizations market their products and services, you quickly learn the two basic types of organizations: *product-driven* and *market-driven*. It is the product-driven firms that typically declare bankruptcy. It is the market-driven firms that become the case studies of how to run a successful business" (George Barna, *A Step-by-Step Guide to Church Marketing: Breaking Ground for the Harvest* [Ventura, Calif.: Regal Books, 1992], p. 26).

2. Shawchuck, Kotler, Wrenn, and Rath, *Marketing for Congregations*, p. 57.

3. See, for example, Philip D. Kenneson, "Worship Wars and Rumors of Worship Wars," *Reviews in Religion and Theology* (May 1996): 72-75.

4. Cf. George Barna, *User Friendly Churches: What Christians Need to Know About the Churches People Love to Go To* (Ventura, Calif.: Regal Books, 1991).

5. Shawchuck, Kotler, Wrenn, and Rath, *Marketing for Congregations*, p. 62.

6. For examples of ways in which Christian people have contributed to the commodification of the Christian faith, see R. Laurence Moore, *Selling God: American Religion in the Marketplace of Culture* (New York: Oxford University Press, 1994).

168

7. Ferdinand Tönnies, *Community and Society*, trans. and ed. Charles P. Loomis (New York: Harper and Row, 1963), p. 252.
8. Shawchuck, Kotler, Wrenn, and Rath, *Marketing for Congregations*, p. 47.
9. Barna, *Step-by-Step Guide*, p. 27.
10. Lyle E. Schaller, *Create Your Own Future!* (Nashville: Abingdon Press, 1992), p. 130. In this same chapter, Schaller draws the distinction even more unhelpfully when he sets in opposition the "tradition-bound" church and the "market-driven" church.
11. Shawchuck, Kotler, Wrenn, and Rath, *Marketing for Congregations*, p. 66.
12. Or as Marva J. Dawn pointedly remarks with respect to the church's worship: "The contemporary demand to find a 'marketing niche' actually threatens genuine Christian community, for the purpose of true worship is to offer to God what will be pleasing to God." See Marva J. Dawn, *Reaching Out Without Dumbing Down: A Theology of Worship for the Turn-of-the-Century Culture* (Grand Rapids: Eerdmans, 1995), p. 130.
13. George Barna, *Marketing the Church* (Colorado Springs, Colo.: NavPress, 1988), p. 37; emphasis added.
14. Shawchuck, Kotler, Wrenn and Rath, *Marketing for Congregations*, pp. 47-48.
15. Barna, *Marketing the Church* p. 36.
16. As Shawchuck et al. remind us: "Value is in the eye of the beholder. It doesn't matter how much value we see in the product we are offering. What matters is the perception of the party whom we wish to engage in exchange" (*Marketing for Congregations*, p. 112). Such unqualified affirmation of "consumer sovereignty" seems hard to rectify with this group's earlier (p. 51) insistence that a congregation's mission "does not include pandering to current popular tastes."
17. Now it is true that church marketers address "whose needs" they are trying to meet when they speak about "positioning." But the way in which this question runs within a marketing approach is precisely the opposite way it should run for churches. To the extent that churches should be concerned about meeting needs, the question should be: What and whose needs will we as a community find ourselves meeting in order to continue to be who we've been called to be? In contrast, the whole premise of "positioning" within marketing is that the proper question is: How do we market ourselves in ways that will clearly present our organization as positioned to meet the specific felt needs of a specific target audience? As the next chapter shows, within the positioning model, the factor that too often shapes the decision to "target" this particular people's needs rather than someone else's needs involves what that group has to offer in exchange. Not surprisingly, in the midst of this concern for positioning, targeting, and exchange, the notion that the church exists to worship and bear witness to the triune God seems to get lost.
18. Barna, *Marketing the Church*, pp. 28, 93.
19. Shawchuck, Kotler, Wrenn, and Rath, *Marketing for Congregations*, p. 89.
20. Ibid., p. 91.
21. Several observers of church life in American society have noticed the ways in which people's loyalties to particular church traditions are changing. For example, many have noted the ways in which denominational loyalty, which was many times rooted in differences in doctrine, seems to be a thing of the past. There might be some cause to celebrate this shift, except what seems to

be replacing it appears even more pernicious. Robert Wuthnow has noted that when Americans choose a church, their choice increasingly reflects a wider political polarization in American society. Others have noted the ways in which people choose a church primarily on the basis of what they call worship "style" or "preference." See Wuthnow, *The Restructuring of American Religion* (Princeton: Princeton University Press, 1988).

22. George Barna, *Finding a Church You Can Call Home: The Complete Guide to Making One of the Most Significant Decisions of Your Life* (Ventura, Calif.: Regal Books, 1992). In this volume, Barna makes clear that as a church shopper "your goal is to choose the best church—the one that will prove most satisfying and will address your needs most effectively" (p. 40).

23. Friedrich Nietzsche, *The Portable Nietzsche* (New York: Penguin Books, 1976), pp. 515-16.

24. Shawchuck, Kotler, Wrenn, and Rath, *Marketing for Congregations*, p. 64.

5. The Baby Boomerang

1. Norman Shawchuck, Philip Kotler, Bruce Wrenn, and Gustave Rath, *Marketing for Congregations: Choosing to Serve People More Effectively* (Nashville: Abingdon Press, 1992), p. 167.

2. George Barna, *A Step-by-Step Guide to Church Marketing: Breaking Ground for the Harvest* (Ventura, Calif.: Regal Books, 1992), pp. 141-42.

3. See, for example, Doug Murren, *The Baby Boomerang: Catching Baby Boomers as They Return to Church* (Ventura, Calif.: Regal Books, 1990). Before quoting this Pauline passage, Murren writes: "Pluralism is a great challenge to the Church in our American culture. The marketing mania of our society has caused our culture to be divided into ever-smaller segments. Each has its own language, and each expects to be catered to. This segmentation process will make our task easier if we in the Church learn to embrace it and accept it is a factor in our ministry" (p. 39).

4. C. René Padilla, "The Unity of the Church and the Homogeneous Unit Principle," in *Exploring Church Growth*, ed. Wilbert R. Shenk (Grand Rapids: Eerdmans, 1983), p. 287. The internal quotation above, that "men like to become Christians without crossing racial, linguistic or class barriers," is a reference to the work of Donald McGavran, who was an early advocate of what has become known as the "homogeneous unit principle." See his *Understanding Church Growth* (Grand Rapids: Eerdmans, 1970), p. 198.

5. Shawchuck, Kotler, Wrenn, and Rath, *Marketing for Congregations*, p. 174.

6. Barna, *A Step-by-Step Guide to Church Marketing*, p. 159.

7. It is significant that the language of "values" is rooted in economic metaphors. As such, value language seems well-suited to the marketplace, since we are commonly encouraged to choose our "values" in ways that seem remarkably parallel to how we make other consumer choices.

8. Barna, *A Step-by-Step Guide to Church Marketing*, pp. 159-60.

9. Ibid., p.160.

10. Shawchuck, Kotler, Wrenn, and Rath, *Marketing for Congregations*, p. 174.

11. Ibid., p. 47. See also their claim that "to perform its mission, the church or synagogue needs to attract resources through exchange" (p. 86).

12. Barna, *A Step-by-Step Guide to Church Marketing*, pp. 160-61.

13. George Barna, *Marketing the Church* (Colorado Springs, Colo.: NavPress, 1988), p. 31.

6. Create Your Own Future!

1. Bryan R. Wilson, "God in Retirement," *The Twentieth Century* 170, 1011 (Autumn 1961): 24.
2. A recent issue of *Time* magazine noted that "some of today's most influential religious figures are no longer theologians but therapists." The article then goes on to note that the guru of the evangelicals is child psychologist James Dobson, while "mainline dropouts and seekers" remain enamored of psychiatrist M. Scott Peck, whose book *The Road Less Traveled* was a *New York Times* best-seller for a record 490 weeks. See "The Church Search," *Time*, 5 April 1993, pp. 44-49.
3. Robert Pattison writes: "By forcing churches to compete on the basis of their ability to titillate the instincts of their worshipers, vulgar pantheism compels the champions of organized religions to abandon their pretensions to superior truth and turns them into entrepreneurs of emotional stimulation. Once God becomes a commodity used for self-gratification, his fortunes depend on the vagaries of the emotional marketplace." See *The Triumph of Vulgarity: Rock Music in the Mirror of Romanticism* (New York: Oxford University Press, 1987), p. 186.
4. George Barna, *Marketing the Church* (Colorado Springs, Colo.: NavPress, 1988), p. 14. Although in some of his writing Lyle E. Schaller appears to agree with many of the presuppositions of church marketers, to his credit he adamantly insists that the church is not a business. See Schaller, *Looking in the Mirror: Self-Appraisal in the Local Church* (Nashville: Abingdon Press, 1984), especially pp. 41-51, where Schaller details twelve important differences between churches and businesses.
5. Norman Shawchuck, Philip Kotler, Bruce Wrenn, and Gustave Rath, *Marketing for Congregations: Choosing to Serve People More Effectively* (Nashville: Abingdon Press, 1992), p. 46.
6. Barna, *Marketing the Church*, p. 44.
7. Alasdair MacIntyre, *After Virtue*, 2nd ed. (Notre Dame, Ind.: University of Notre Dame Press, 1984), p. 77.
8. George Barna, *A Step-by-Step Guide to Church Marketing: Breaking Ground for the Harvest* (Ventura, Calif.: Regal Books, 1992), p. 44.
9. Shawchuck, Kotler, Wrenn, and Rath, *Marketing for Congregations*, p. 86.
10. Robert E. Stevens and David L. Loudon, *Marketing for Churches and Ministries* (New York: Haworth Press, 1992), pp. 8-9.
11. Shawchuck, Kotler, Wrenn, and Rath, *Marketing for Congregations*, pp. 394, 395.
12. Stevens and Loudon, *Marketing for Churches and Ministries*, p. 58.
13. Ibid., p. 58.
14. Barna, *Marketing the Church*, p. 100.
15. Barna, *A Step-by-Step Guide*, pp. 174, 327.
16. Interview with George Barna, *Leadership* (Summer 1995): 123-24.
17. Eric W. Gritsch and Robert W. Jenson, *Lutheranism: The Theological Movement and Its Confessional Writings* (Philadelphia: Fortress Press, 1976), pp. 204-5. We are indebted to Inagrace T. Dietterich for leading us to this refer-

ence. See her article, "Toward a Faithful and Effective Ecclesiology," *Modern Theology* 9 (October 1993): 349-68.

18. There are, of course, many other "management" techniques that Christians are tempted to use as a means of imposing order. For example, Thomas G. Long, in an insightful editorial about the questionable theological presuppositions underwriting the administration and use of the personality test known as the Myers-Briggs Type Indicator (MBTI), rightly notes that "like many other explanatory schemes that have become popular in pastoral circles—faith development, the stages of dying, and the categories of congregational growth, to name some others—the MBTI grid of personality types is an attempt to make manageable what is essentially unpredictable, to force some semblance of order onto a process that is inescapably wild and full of wondrous surprises." See "Myers-Briggs and Other Modern Astrologies," *Theology Today* 49, 3 (October 1992): 295.

19. Barna, *Marketing the Church*, pp. 34-35.

20. Interview with George Barna, *Leadership* (Summer 1995): 123.

21. Robert D. Lupton, *Theirs Is the Kingdom: Celebrating the Gospel in Urban America* (San Francisco: HarperCollins, 1989), p. 91.

22. Shawchuck, Kotler, Wrenn, and Rath, *Marketing for Congregations*, p. 45.

23. Claire Watkins has helped us formulate this way of stating the matter. She makes a slightly different point in her essay, "The Church as a 'Special' Case: Comments from Ecclesiology Concerning the Management of the Church," *Modern Theology* 9 (October 1993): 369-84.

24. Of course, managing by objective is not the only possible management model, although it is a popular one among many church marketers. For example, total quality management eschews the setting of objectives because doing so makes an organization *less* responsive. Not surprisingly, Christians have already begun thinking about the implications of this new form of management for the church. See, for example, Walt Kallestad and Steven Schey, *Total Quality Ministry* (Minneapolis: Augsburg Fortress, 1994); Norman Shawchuck, *Benchmarks of Quality in the Church: 21 Ways to Continuously Improve the Content of Your Ministry* (Nashville: Abingdon Press, 1994); and Ezra Earl Jones, *Quest for Quality in the Church: A New Paradigm* (Nashville: Discipleship Resources, 1993).

25. Stevens and Loudon, *Marketing for Churches and Ministries*, p. 62.

26. Barna, *Marketing the Church*, p. 14.

27. Ibid., p. 157.

28. Many church marketers work hard to distance themselves and their approach from "church growth" approaches. For example, one group of marketers insists that their approach does not emphasize growth, but quality; growth is only a by-product of quality. They write: "While both church growth and financial growth have important roles to play in the church or synagogue, marketing is neither. *Marketing is a discipline intended to address the development of quality congregations and ministries. . . .* Developing quality congregations usually will lead to church growth and financial growth, but as a by-product rather than as the essential goal" (see Shawchuck, Kotler, Wrenn, and Rath, *Marketing for Congregations*, p. 32). While we are heartened to see this group of marketers distance themselves from the notion of "growth for growth's sake," they continue to encourage the view that numerical growth is a valid indicator of success. For example, only a few pages after

172

the above disclaimer about "growth," these marketers say the following under the heading "What Are the Common Characteristics of Successful Congregations?": "There are some congregations of every size and in every ecclesiastical body that are *characterized by growth and expanding ministries*" (p. 37, italics added). Hence, success is characterized not by faithfulness or even by "quality ministry," but by growth and expansion. We believe much of the current interest in church marketing stems from its promises to deliver growth as a by-product if churches focus on "quality." Said another way, church marketers may be no less interested in growth than are more traditional "church growth" advocates, but they are savvy enough to realize that in a market-oriented society, one cannot hope to achieve growth without entering into exchanges that will result in growth as a highly desirable "by-product."

29. William H. Willimon, *Acts* (Atlanta: John Knox Press, 1988), p. 105.
30. Alasdair MacIntyre offers considerable help in seeing through the pretensions of "effectiveness." He rightly suggests that the effectiveness of the manager is usually an imputed effectiveness: "That the notion [of effectiveness] is used to sustain and extend the authority and power of managers is not of course in question; but its use in connection with those tasks derives from the belief that managerial authority and power are justified because managers possess an ability to put skills and knowledge to work in the service of achieving certain ends. But what if effectiveness were not a quality widely imputed to managers and bureaucrats both by themselves and others, but in fact a quality which rarely exists apart from this imputation?" See *After Virtue*, p. 75.
31. Shawchuck, Kotler, Wrenn, and Rath, *Marketing for Congregations*, p. 68.
32. Lyle E. Schaller, *Create Your Own Future!* (Nashville: Abingdon Press, 1991), p. 88.
33. Shawchuck, Kotler, Wrenn, and Rath, *Marketing for Congregations*, p. 21.
34. Dietterich, "Toward a Faithful and Effective Ecclesiology," p. 350.

7. The Responsive Congregation

1. For a clear example of the centrality of this concept to the church marketing enterprise, see the chapter, "Serving People Effectively: The Responsive Congregation," in Norman Shawchuck, Philip Kotler, Bruce Wrenn, and Gustave Rath, *Marketing for Congregations: Choosing to Serve People More Effectively* (Nashville: Abingdon Press, 1992), pp. 67-78.
2. Ibid., p. 38.
3. Ibid., p. 68, italics added.
4. Shawchuck, et al., offer a responsiveness continuum for "consumer-response organizations." This continuum runs from unresponsive, through casually and highly responsive, to fully responsive. The descriptions and examples the authors give of each type make it clear that the more responsive a congregation is, the more "effective and satisfying" its ministry will be for both those ministering and those ministered to (ibid., p. 78).
5. Ibid., p. 136, italics added.
6. Ibid., p. 87.
7. Ibid., p. 87.
8. Ibid., p. 89.

173

9. See ibid., p. 91, where the authors write: "The mission should also be motivational. Those working for the organization should feel that they are worthwhile members of a worthwhile endeavor. A congregation whose mission includes helping the poor is likely to inspire more support than one whose mission is meeting the social, cultural, and athletic needs of its current members. The mission should be something that enriches people's lives."

10. For a powerful exposition of this point, see Gerhard Lohfink's fine work *Jesus and Community: The Social Dimension of Christian Faith* (Philadelphia: Fortress Press, 1984).

11. George Barna, *Marketing the Church* (Colorado Springs, Colo.: NavPress, 1988), p. 45.

12. George Lindbeck, "The Sectarian Future of the Church," in *The God Experience: Essays in Hope*, ed. Joseph P. Whelan, S.J. (New York: Paulist Press, 1971), p. 227.

13. Martin Marty, as quoted in Kenneth L. Woodward, "Dead End for the Mainline?" *Newsweek*, 9 August 1993, p. 48.

14. Up to this point in our argument we have seen how church marketing is steeped in the modernist project. Its pursuit of control, its naive view of "data," its attempts at predicting and managing the future all take their cue from a certain way of understanding the world and our place in it bequeathed to us, first by science and now, more important, by the social sciences. Moreover, in almost every case church marketing exalts the new over the old, the large over the small, the present over the past, experience over memory, innovation over tradition, change over continuity, ease over difficulty, and measurement over discernment.

15. This impact of consumption on identity has been articulated powerfully by Richard Harvey Brown, who writes:

Instead of people choosing things, things now choose people, in the sense of defining their identities. When people buy designer clothes, for example, they are paying for the look and label, and in so doing they acquire an identity as that sort of person. Similarly, smoking a certain cigarette is associated with cowboys or canoeing; using a certain menstrual napkin is presented as liberating one for skydiving or gymnastics. Even those displeased with advanced capitalism display their protest against it by shifting to alternative purchases, thereby reaffirming the assumption that self and value are defined by consumption. Daily life becomes a kind of manic propitiation to the products/gods that determine our identities/destinies. Yet these products, though they have a magical power to suggest an image of the self, do not in fact convey an integral identity. And how could they, since the items to be purchased are substitutable according to stylistic affinities and imminent obsolescence? As with cars, modes of leisure, dress, and pleasure, so the distinction between alternative modes of being is always within a limited and exterior universe of meaning—that of alternative "life-styles."

See *Society as Text: Essays on Rhetoric, Reason, and Reality* (Chicago: University of Chicago Press, 1987), p. 46.

16. See Robert Wuthnow, *Sharing the Journey: Support Groups and America's New Quest for Community* (New York: The Free Press, 1994), pp. 194-97.

17. Barna, *Marketing the Church*, p. 23.
18. Barna, *Marketing the Church*, p. 14.
19. Shawchuck, Kotler, Wrenn, and Rath, *Marketing for Congregations*, p. 112.
20. We are unsure when this language first became popular, but it was given an enormous boost by the widely read book by Lee Strobel, *Inside the Mind of Unchurched Harry and Mary* (Grand Rapids: Zondervan, 1993).
21. Quoted in Shawchuck, Kotler, Wrenn, and Rath, *Marketing for Congregations*, p. 408.
22. Stanley Hauerwas and William H. Willimon, *Resident Aliens* (Nashville: Abingdon Press, 1989), p. 78. As the authors note later on, being a minister in a market-driven society (let alone a market-driven congregation) is an exercise in frustration that often results in self-loathing: "If the ministry is reduced to being primarily a helping profession then those who take up that office cannot help being destroyed if they have any integrity. For they will find themselves frustrated by a people not trained on the narrative of God's salvation, not trained to want the right things rightly, but rather a people who share the liberal presumption that all needs which are sincerely felt are legitimate. . . . Pastors come to despise what they are and to hate the community that made them that way. Because the church is not a place to worship God, but a therapeutic center for the meeting of one another's unchecked, unexamined needs, the pastor is exhausted. . . . One of the reasons some church members are so mean-spirited with their pastor, particularly when the pastor urges them to look at God, is that they feel deceived by such pastoral invitations to look beyond themselves. They have come to church for 'strokes,' to have their personal needs met. Whence all this pulpit talk about 'finding our lives by losing them'?" (pp. 121, 124, 138).
23. William H. Willimon, *The Intrusive Word* (Nashville: Abingdon Press, 1994), p. 22.
24. Shawchuck, Kotler, Wrenn, and Rath, *Marketing for Congregations*, p. 48.
25. Walter Brueggemann, *Biblical Perspectives on Evangelism: Living in a Three-Storied Universe* (Nashville: Abingdon Press, 1993), p. 88.
26. See Lyle Schaller, *Choices for Churches* (Nashville: Abingdon Press, 1990), p. 70, where he argues that those who critique the homogeneous unit principle tend "to be more ideological than pragmatic," as if pragmatism were not itself an ideology. It is telling that Schaller's entire discussion of the church's choice to be either homogeneous or pluralistic is couched in the language of "preference," as if this is just one more issue about which a congregation must decide what it prefers.
27. C. René Padilla, "The Unity of the Church and the Homogeneous Unit Principle," in *Exploring Church Growth*, ed. Wilbert R. Shenk (Grand Rapids: Eerdmans, 1983), p. 301.
28. Barna, *Marketing the Church*, pp. 151-52.
29. Karl Barth, *Church Dogmatics* IV.2 (Edinburgh: T. & T. Clark, 1958), p. 668.
30. Padilla, "The Unity of the Church and the Homogeneous Unit Principle," pp. 301-2, italics added. Both we and Padilla borrow from John Poulton the notion of the church as an embodied question mark. In commenting on the early church's impact on the surrounding society, Poulton wrote: "When masters could call slaves brothers, and when the enormities of depersonalizing them became conscious in enough people's minds, something had to go. It took time, but slavery went. And in the interim, the people of God were

an embodied question-mark because here were some people who could live another set of relationships within the given social system." See *People Under Pressure* (London: Lutterworth Press, 1973), p. 112.

31. More than one commentator has noted how the language of "character" is more closely tied to issues of production, while the language of "personality" fits well with consumption. See Brown, *Society as Text*, pp. 46-47; and Warren Susman, "Personality and the Making of Twentieth-Century Culture," in *New Directions in American Intellectual History*, eds. John Higham and Paul K. Conkin (Baltimore: Johns Hopkins University Press, 1979), pp. 212-26.

32. Cf. Marva J. Dawn, *Reaching Out Without Dumbing Down*.

33. Willimon, *The Intrusive Word* , pp. 18, 19, 22.

34. William H. Willimon, "Preaching: Entertainment or Exposition?"*Christian Century* 107 (Feb. 28, 1990): 206.

35. For example, one group of church marketers writes: "The good news is that every church and synagogue, large and small, might make itself more appealing, relevant, and sensitive to its constituents and its environment without compromising its mission. Marketing can assist these congregations, large and small, to accomplish that goal." See Shawchuck, Kotler, Wrenn, and Rath, *Marketing for Congregations*, p. 31.

Conclusion: The Man Nobody Knows

1. Gordon D. Fee, *The First Epistle to the Corinthians*, The New International Commentary on the New Testament (Grand Rapids: Eerdmans, 1987), p. 145. We are indebted to Fee's analysis for our reflections on these Pauline passages.

2. See Norman Shawchuck, Philip Kotler, Bruce Wrenn, and Gustave Rath, *Marketing for Congregations: Choosing to Serve People More Effectively* (Nashville: Abingdon Press, 1992), p. 316, for this striking phrase.

3. Bruce Barton, *The Man Nobody Knows: A Discovery of the Real Jesus* (New York: Bobbs-Merrill, 1924). Barton concludes his introduction ("How It Came to Be Written"), with a story about a man who had discovered the "real Jesus": " 'Some day,' said he, 'some one will write a book about Jesus. Every business man will read it and send it to his partners and his salesmen. For it will tell the story of the founder of modern business.' So the man waited for some one to write the book, but no one did. Instead, more books were published about the 'lamb of God' who was weak and unhappy and glad to die. The man became impatient. One day he said, 'I believe I will try to write that book myself.' And he did."